SPIRITUALLY WAKING UP

You (SERIOUSLY) Can't Make This Sh*t Up

LISA ANN

AM2U, LLC
www.AngelMessages2U.com

Printed Worldwide
First Printing 2023
First Edition 2023

10 9 8 7 6 5 4 3 2 1

DISCLAIMER NOTICE

DEDICATION

To my great-aunt and grandparents on the other side: Your help, support and messages through this journey have, and continue to be, hugely instrumental in my growth. There truly aren't enough words. Thank you for making me laugh and proving to me over and over that you are indeed around.

To Dorothy: I can't tell you how much your messages have meant to me while I mended my heart. Thank you for coming through time and time again and tattling. I am grateful.

To the original Woo-Woo Super Friends Group: Thank you all for participating in and being a safe group to share ongoing experiences with.

To Agent 007: Your support and belief in me have been appreciated in more ways than I can count. Thank you!

To Cathy G.: Thank you for being such a good friend and being supportive no matter how crazy the stories were. May we continue solving world problems over sushi forever.

TABLE OF CONTENTS

PROLOGUE

FIRST UP, ME: THE GOOD, BAD, AND THE UGLY.

Be yourself; Everyone else is already taken.

— Oscar Wilde.

My "council" (aka my spirit guide) is commissioning me to write. We all are on our own spiritual journey, and this is mine.

Where I am right now is that half of me wants to hide in the little bubble I have created. It's quite cozy in here! Then, there is this ever-so-small (right now) part of me that is ready to sneak back into life. You know what I'm talking about. It's that "hold-your-nose-as-you-jump-in-the-deep-end" side. Or as Nike's slogan states: *Just Do It.*

So, who am I? I am like everyone else—well sort of. As we all have stories, let me give you the cliffs notes version.

THE GOOD: I would say that I am a loyal, hardworking mother of two adorable young men. I am an excellent listener. Quite often, I channel my inner five-year-old and have been known to stick my tongue out, giggle at inappropriate things, and make decisions based on the rock, paper, scissors game. I have to practice speaking with a filter. Most definitely, a leader. That "take charge" side steps out in full force sometimes. Unofficially, I have labeled myself Camp Counselor at Camp Wannahockaloogie. Definitely competitive at times but mostly with myself. Sincerely love audiobooks, cutting the grass, walking in the woods, and scuba diving. I cheer on the underdog! (Former cheerleader, thank you very much!) As with all women, and people in general, there are many layers to me. Depending on what the moment calls for, is how I show up. Most often I'm the glass-half-full kind of gal!

THE BAD & UGLY: Ugh. I don't think there is enough time or computer space to admit everything. So, before I let you know about some of my vulnerable, soft underbelly, let me preface this with I-AM-HUMAN and SO-ARE-YOU. Although there are some people who like to feel superior based on some unknown "rule book," the reality is: There isn't a rule book. We are all students of life. That being said, I am sure that there could be many additions and subtractions to my list based on who you speak to.

Here is my version: I have what I call tunnel vision syndrome. If I'm on a quest, the world can pass me by. I only see one thing and one thing only. Let's see, I have no patience with myself. I want to know something like the back of my hand right now. Not in baby steps. I suffer the affliction of giving way too many chances to some and none to others.

Most times, I'm a "multitasker extraordinaire." Except when it comes to yin and yang; sometimes I am all yin and others all yang. Balance? Nope! Still working on that.

One more tarnished tangent of mine is that, on occasion, I need to wear the sign: DOES NOT PLAY WELL WITH OTHERS. The translation is: I need to regroup, reset, and retreat. I can go from being a tornado to turtle mode in about two days. Watch out when I am in tornado mode! Two weeks' worth of work can get done in a day. Just about the time you get your sneakers tied to join me, I can be in turtle mode.

Now you know! So, if you see me write something that seems off-kilter, you will at least have a hint of where I am coming from. I reserve the right to add to my list when I deem fit in any of the good, bad, or ugly categories.

I also write like I talk. Well, to be honest, I am probably cleaning up the necessary things to make this readable. Truly, though, if you talk to me in person sometime, I can be short and sweet and straight to the point or as some call me—blunt. Yet other times, flowery, sweet, and using every descriptive adjective out there. Some of you are going to get me and others won't. I won't be upset. I appreciate the opportunity to show my personality.

Let's cut to the chase. Why write this book? Whelp, there is a lot to this, but basically, I was asked to. By whom? Jean-Paul Claude, whom I affectionately (and with permission) call "JP." Who is he? One of my guardian angels. The reason JP asked me to write this is that I have a funny way of looking at life that many—hopefully all—of you will relate to.

A couple of miscellaneous disclaimers: Lots of cool stories have already happened that I will share here. Some you will believe, and there might be a few that stem outside your realm of imaginable. IT'S OK. My favorite slogan is YOU CAN'T MAKE THIS SHIT UP! I do swear every so often so if that doesn't work for you, stop reading now!

I am an advocate of giving credit where credit is due. Seriously, I am not a name-dropper to impress anyone but the names that I do drop of a teacher, school, business, or other are because they impressed me.

I also am an advocate for privacy. There might be a story I write about here that I am privy to on my journey. It is not my intent to make fun of or underplay the seriousness of anyone's situation, request, or story. I might find a funny spin on it. It's my spin. Life and situations are not all rainbows, unicorns, and butterflies. I cry, get upset, and channel my inner three-year-old temper tantrums at times!

I also have my very own soapbox. (Don't be a hater! I bet you have your very own too!) I won't have to mention it—you will know it when you see it.

I will be changing names and places to protect privacy. Any similarity to your own experience or story is purely coincidental. I am not here to pass judgment or victim-shame anyone. You have your own free will. This is *my* path, *my* truth, and I am sincerely grateful if I can help you in some way, shape, or form by example.

This is a collection of stories about my spiritual journey to further enlightenment. Over time, my growth and approach change the more I learn. I am very respectful of my spirit guides. We all have a sense of humor though.

They spend a lot of time trying to lighten me up in more ways than one! I am not perfect. I don't know it all but I'm well on my way. So, sit back, grab some popcorn, and enjoy the ride!

CHAPTER 1

GIVE IT TO THE PAPER – JOURNALING AS THERAPY

Once upon a time, there seemed to be so much going on in my brain that I did everything I could to avoid the constant internal dialogue. My brain became so full of things to analyze that I stopped listening. So much so, that I intentionally made my life noisy so that I didn't have to listen to it. I just flat-out refused. Should I have a moment of pause, my brain would take it as an open invitation to say, "Let's talk." I didn't want to deal with it.

I found myself going to bed every night listening to the eleven o'clock news. My goal was to be out cold before the sports report came on at twenty after the hour. Sleeping became a stress relief. I jokingly told everybody that I would only be able to "dumb down" and finally sleep if I had noise around to distract my brain.

Yeah, that only worked for a little while until I said out loud, "I'm afraid of what my brain is going to tell me." No truer words were said then that statement. Think of a five-year-old sticking their fingers in their ears going, "La la la la, I can't hear you. La la la …" That was me.

Then, I got to the point where I started leaning on my friends because of the mental build-up. My mental state was on autopilot and a nonstop rotation of the same shit, different day. My conversations were repeating with no resolution. Most friends can only handle a discussion about the same thing over and over again for so long. I saw the strain in my friendships, and it bothered me.

So, I stopped talking to my friends about my tangent of the moment. Rightfully so, I could tell they didn't want to listen anyway. They had their own lives and issues to deal with. I retreated inward even more, consistently bottling up everything inside even tighter. I couldn't seem to wrap my own head around what was going on, let alone find a solution, except to circle around the drain for the millionth time.

I got to the point where the stress level and unhappiness of everything that was going on outside and inside were colliding and I started to crack along the edges. Finally, it got to the point that, if my brain knew that I was calm for even five minutes, it would say, "Oh, good. Now that you're sitting still, let's go over everything that you've been avoiding." The internal conflict inside of me had gotten worse and was now interrupting my sleep. It was the only time I could listen to my higher self.

Feeling as if I had finally found a potential solution, it came to me to "give it to the paper." That seemed to be a logical action to take. I finally had to resign myself that if I give it to the lined white sheets of whatever notepad I had next to my bed, the paper would hold my never-ending to-do list, thoughts and suggestions for me until morning. I'm sure this was born of my love of making lists.

I noticed I was making multiple lists. Sometimes even lists for the lists! I took great pride in crossing thoughts and jobs off, but even that wasn't enough anymore. Something was still missing. I needed to express myself.

Eventually, I realized I couldn't write every single thing that was going on in my brain on my paper because it wasn't meant for anybody else's eyes. At the time, I had a husband and two little boys who needed attention, and my desire to build a small empire in the real estate industry had me constantly at the wheel and foot on the gas pedal.

I got to the point where I wasn't happy. The cracks were getting bigger, and the flood of emotions were starting to come through. I did not understand how to deal with my emotions. There wasn't anybody I could talk to and no place that I could turn, to really just dump everything that was building up behind the dam causing it to crack. My husband didn't know how to help me because I wouldn't talk to him. Many mornings I would get in my car to go to work and start crying. The mask of superwoman I put on for the world was falling and I couldn't keep up the charade of being happy all the time. It was affecting every part of my life. I needed help. Nonjudgmental help.

I needed to talk and get my jumbled feelings out in some way without prying eyes over my shoulder or dealing with well-meaning opinions from others. It had to be private and yet accessible whenever I needed it. It had to be available to me during the day, night or wherever I was when traveling.

I stumbled across wordpress.com and promptly created an online journal. It was here that I could write, swear, and be completely raw about how I was feeling. I didn't need to sugar-coat what I typed because it was for my eyes only. It gave me the opportunity to hash out the same subject repeatedly, ultimately saving face, because no one else knew. I needed to sort through my intense and unrealized feelings and thoughts on many subjects.

I start every journal with the same opening statement. *This is where I'm at, the day I write. It does not mean that where I am at is a fixed state of being. It's just me trying to deal with what is going on in my brain at that moment.* I only say this because, heaven forbid, someone should read it or get hold of it and interpret my words or twist them to imply something else.

So, I started "giving it to the paper" by typing. Boy, did my fingers fly! It was like drawing blood; once you've popped the vein, it just free flowed.

Nobody was going to see what I wrote, so I wrote every detail of every thought like I was telling my best friend. I wrote and did not hold anything back. I typed every single gory detail—every twist, turn, nook, and cranny. I spared no detail.

I realized I had a distinct need to just get it out of my system. It was a primary need of mine at that moment. I also needed to know that it went someplace where I would never be judged by prying eyes who might try to interpret my mental state at that time. It gave me a new breath of life.

There would be times I would write five to ten times a day. It was easier than picking up the phone to talk to someone every single time some wild thought crossed my brain. I fully embraced the idea of saying every single thing, about anything, without judgment. No matter when the thought crossed my mind, my journal was available to receive whatever I dumped into it. After all, nobody would ever see it except me.

I wasn't nice. In fact, I was very raw, blunt and to the point. I've often joked that if anyone ever found my journal, I would need to go into a witness protection program. I've even gone so far as to code-name people, places, and events. Should anything by accident be discovered, the anonymity of those involved in my life was protected.

Simply put, what I wrote is how I felt in that moment about whatever I was going through.

Eighteen-plus years later, and more gigabytes than I probably care to admit, I am shocked and awed that I am not being charged by some governmental agency for the tremendous number of characters that I have written over the years.

There are certain moments when I have looked back and read things from months or years ago. I see my mental state and thought process at the time and how much it has changed over the years. The amount of energy that I have poured into the details has become more severe and lessened all at the same time. What was once important is no longer. Yet other things are more important now too.

It's been an incredible journey for me to write. Although going back and rereading is sometimes exhilarating because of some of the stuff that I have written, it is also like ripping off a Band-Aid. You are not meant to recall all the intense details that can be written on a moment-by-moment basis. You are meant to learn lessons, to understand where you're coming from, and hopefully understand why, so you can move forward.

I've often joked that at some point, if I get really bored in my future, I could reread my entire life's adventures. I have revealed some of the most painstaking details and my innermost thoughts that I wouldn't even share with some of my closest friends and relations.

Writing has been my therapy. Writing has been my savior. People talk about journaling all the time and want to know how to get started. I often just say start! I encourage you to write like you're going to tell your best friend who you know will *never* say a word.

You can give wherever you write its own name, so that when you say, "I'm going to write a letter to (blank)," you do. Write every detail, thought, twist and triumph.

When you hit save, set it to private, and walk away. If you prefer the paper and pen style, simply close the book.

I do realize that if, for some reason, the entire Internet system crashed and it was deleted, many years of my life history would be erased in the blink of an eye. At this point, I understand myself so much better that I don't know that I need it.

Simply put, I write.

As of late, I have discovered talk dictation on my phone. This option allows me to verbally just lay it all out there as if I am talking with a friend. It is wonderful because I can talk in the car, which is sometimes the only alone time I might have. Doing it on the run also can save me time as I need not be stationary in front of a computer.

I suggest that you keep your journal and its contents to yourself. You don't need to prove anything to anybody, and it is truly meant for your eyes only. It is there if you need to reference how you felt and why. It's also very enlightening to see how you change and evolve through the lessons that you have learned. I will warn you though, when and if you ever look back at it, some of it might be cringeworthy. Honor your feelings and don't be so hard on yourself if you do. Again, it was where you were. Of course, if you see patterns not yet resolved, well, you have a good starting place to work on yourself.

Journaling this way has allowed me to sleep better. In fact, I've even let go of the need to create lists, with a few exceptions. I also no longer feel the need to tell everybody my business. I write or talk, hit save, and put it away. I am only writing to myself. I have truly learned to become my own best friend.

Journaling has allowed me to see a 360° view of life and the challenges that I have faced. It has saved many friendships. Until I got the words right, I could circle the drain as long as I needed to with no pressure.

Not everybody is happy all the time. Everyone is concerned about themselves and their own lives, which they should be! Because I journal, it has kept gossiping ammunition to disrupt my life away from well-meaning friends.

What I have found is that writing has been very therapeutic for me. Besides having the ability to vent and take out my frustrations, writing without a filter made me learn about myself on a journey that I didn't even realize I was on.

Grab your pen and notepad or turn on your computer—remembering to set it to private—and write. Then let it go. It is much cheaper and faster than therapy.

History is yesterday, but it may help you understand who you are today.

Chapter 2

What You See Is What You Get

While I was waiting patiently for the stars to align before I could move, I was listening to various self-help type books and programs. I rendered them my own pep squad at times. Who I listened to depended on where I was mentally and spiritually at the time. One of the things that I still listen to on occasion is *The Secret*. One of the people in that video discussed putting a vision board together and how he currently lived in the exact house he put on his board five years prior.

One day, after all my household chores were done, I got the nudge to put together my own vision board. Cutting out pictures and putting them on a poster board was not the problem. What I needed to figure out was what pictures I wanted to put on this board. That had me thinking, a *lot*. Seriously, what exactly did I want? Sound easy? Nope! Not at first.

You know, ultimately, it was a big question to ponder for me. I was grateful as it was, with what I had. My angels were working their magic in front and behind the scenes. I had a roof over my head, my bills were paid, I had clothes in my closet and food in the refrigerator. I truly had the basics.

I wasn't quite sure how to put my desire for sanity from stress in a picture, but trust me, I was thinking!

The next biggest wish was that the time fairies would hurry the hell up and get my divorce finalized. I wasn't sure what picture to put on my board for that request, either. It did make me ponder for a bit. What exactly did I want now that I was going to be single again?

The rules of vision boarding are that you put out to the universe what you want and visualize seeing yourself with the request.

When you feel like you are drowning, the things you want and need the most are the things that will infuse air into your lungs and give you life again. I wanted more air. A lot more air.

I gave thought to what, and how, I wanted the next phase in my life to look like. No more treading water. I wanted to live again. It wasn't just the big picture I needed to envision, but I also had to figure out what the different components looked like in this new life.

I took to the Internet. After all, it is the world's biggest catalog! Once I found what I wanted, I would take a screenshot of the item and save it to a file on my computer. When I was done, I would send them to the local store, and they would print them for me in an hour. The only rule I gave myself was that if it was tangible I was not allowed to settle. It had to be as close as possible to the exact thing. This made me really dig in. Price was no object.

I found the house I desired and the furniture I wanted to furnish it with. I had pictures of a new bike, clothes, and diving trips to a few different destinations still on my list to see, like the underwater museum in Cancun. I also put pictures of specific experiences I wanted to have, such as being part of a paper lantern festival, seeing hot air balloons at night and seeing the aurora borealis while sleeping in a clear igloo.

I emailed the pictures of everything I wanted to be developed in one hour. After I picked them up, I got my glue, scissors, and poster board out, cranked the tunes and got to cutting and pasting.

TA-DA! My vision board was done. I put a date on it and left it out to look at every day. A few of my friends were curious about what I put on it, but I made no apologies. It was my vision board.

A few months had gone by, and things were steadily progressing toward my move. I decided to see the dermatologist one last time before I went. I was escorted to the exam room and in there was a very colorful bike! Again, in a doctor's exam room. I know lots of people are on health kicks, so it's possible that she rode the bike to work. Shouldn't it be in her office? If nothing else, it was a great conversation piece! It didn't appear to be her aesthetic, though.

She greeted me and I commented on her bike. She said that it was a gift from another patient of hers. Then she said she didn't particularly care for the bike as it was not her style and *did I want it?* My jaw dropped open. (You can't make this shit up!) It happened that fast!

Of course, I said yes! I offered to pay her, but she insisted I would be doing *her* a favor to just take it. It is not something she would use, and she did not want it. She was grateful to have received it but didn't care for the style.

She literally helped me put it in my car and off I went. I explained to her that I had an extremely similar bike on my vision board at home! As a believer in manifesting, she asked me to send her a picture of it, which I did.

Holy cow! Vision boards work!

There are currently ten more things I have checked off that vision board already: specific outfits, dive trips to the exact destinations, cabin trips, my curio cabinet, and more.

A few months ago, I decided to do a more updated board with NEW things in addition to my first board. I very specifically cut out maps of a general area where I wanted to live, found more items to support a new lifestyle and even wrote a check to cash.

The key is to envision yourself with what you desire or wish to experience, then send the wishes off to the universe. Board number two, done. They reside on my nightstand, so I look at them regularly.

Seriously, who would think that you would go into a dermatologist's office and come out with a brand-new free bike? Score! Most places only give you a fancy band-aid or a sucker!

So, I am thinking for a new twist this year, instead of New Year's resolutions, create a board of what you want to see, do, or accomplish. Want to pay off a credit card?

White out a statement and put big zeros and paid in full across it! Be creative! Most importantly, see in your mind that you already have it! After all, what you see is what you get, so make it good!

CHAPTER 3

EVER WANTED TO PICK UP YOUR LIFE AND GO?

Well, I did!

Raise your hand if you have ever just wanted to pick up your life and start over. Like, not even knowing where, when, or how—but just to *go*. A fresh start. A new perspective. New.

Hey! Me too! Guess what? I could, so I did!

Once upon a time, not that long ago, I decided to do just that. My divorce was final, and I needed to just breathe. Heal. Get *me* back—but also figure out who this *me* was. There was light at the end of the tunnel, and I wanted *a lot more light in my life*! I had no idea where I was going to go. Ever just fly by the seat of your pants? You know, one of those moments when you don't have an exact destination but just go somewhere? This was one of those moments for me.

I had three US states that I wanted to investigate.

I got on the computer and gave thought to my new and improved list of non-negotiables. Like Santa, I was makin' a list and checkin' it twice! The list was divided into needs and wants. I got my newly acquired maps out (for a bigger perspective than a computer screen) and looked, viewing things from the big-picture standpoint. Based on all the traveling I had done, I needed to see what resonated the most with me and just listen to my gut. Although I wasn't completely sure what exactly that feeling was supposed to feel like, I just paid attention. My left-brain business side kicked in and I was able to look, research, and at least have a vague game plan. My list was a compilation of states, cities, and addresses to check out neighborhoods in. I consulted a few trusted friends about how they knew about big decisions, and I was told you will just know. UGH. What the *hell* does that mean?

Road Trip! Have-car, will-travel! Off I went. I put some tunes on and started driving. Onward, James! I have read books and seen movies where people have done this. I knew I could do it too. I wasn't exactly sure how, but (those of you that like Chris Farley from *SNL* would understand this), if I had to live in a van down by the river, *I would*.

I covered a lot of ground in just two days. When you know, you know. I looked at apartments, the surroundings, and decided if I felt safe or not. I was making swift progress but decided to call it a night in one city in North Carolina, outside of Raleigh. I secured my sleeping arrangements for the night, did some work remotely, and planned to start fresh in the area to check out the addresses on the list. Liking what I saw in the city, I had a good feeling about the surroundings and moved it to the top of the list.

I put it out to my angels that if this was a place to call home, to show me a sunflower, either in a word or a picture, before I left the city. The next morning, I checked out of the hotel and stopped to grab a bite to eat before getting back on the road. That's when I noticed I had a nail in my tire. (Insert dramatic music here, *dun, dun, DUUUNNN!*)

I went to a tire repair shop that was walking distance from where I was eating, but they did not have the appropriate lug nuts to take my tire off. So, I got on the phone and made calls to other tire places. One said they had what I needed and gave me the address. I said prayers that my car would make the five-mile trek without my tire going flat.

Driving there was like a breath of fresh air! The trees were all in colorful bloom everywhere I looked. It was like how manicured it is on Disney property. It is *that* well-kept. Anyway, the shop owners were extremely pleasant and accommodating. They dropped what they were doing to help me and invited me to sit in the waiting room. I felt great! Everyone was so nice. I just stood there and chatted with some of the guys as they were going in and out of the shop area. I popped a piece of bubble gum in my mouth and looked for a trash can to throw away my wrapper. That's when I saw it.

There was a mural on the wall behind me. Let me stress it was a full wall mural in a tire shop. Again, a *tire shop* wall with a sunflower on it.

A sunflower-in a tire shop! What does a woman holding a basket of sunflowers have to do with *tires*? Not. A. Thing.

Here's your sign.

I was so overwhelmed by the course of events that showed me this sign. First, the nail in the tire and the close tire shop not having the necessary tools? Then, I was forced to find another shop that ultimately led me to the sign I sought. It was the "you just know" along with the black-and-white in-your-face answer. How could I miss the sign I was asking for, now?

I felt so fantastic. I had not trusted that gut feeling alone, but I asked for a sign as a backup and got it. Honestly, the only thing blunter would have been a neon sign!

I had found my new home. I ended up staying for two more nights in the town before I put in an application for my new apartment complex and was approved. Through another course of mishaps, I was assigned an even larger garage than I expected for less money. I just couldn't stop saying, "Thank you."

I drove back to my old home, bypassing the rest of the stops on my list, put my house on the market, had two contracts in ten days, and got exactly what I asked for. My move was seamless.

I was truly grateful. It was meant to be. Ask and you shall receive. I eagerly wait to see what signs my angels provide for me on this next adventure in my new place!

CHAPTER 4

HERMIT NO MORE

The next few weeks were a whirlwind for me in a big way. I had finalized packing and shipped my stuff off to North Carolina. It's a very eye-opening task to not only make major decisions about your life but move out of state, and I help people do this for a living!

The closing for the sale of my home was seamless, but my nerves were shot. I got in the car with one suitcase, a camping chair, blowup air mattress, and drove to North Carolina to my new, but very empty, apartment. Not having kept up with any news or weather because of my schedule, I barely had the car engine off when my kids informed me that a hurricane was headed right toward me. *Sigh* My sons were not happy and told me to get my butt back to Florida. So, what did I do? I got *back* in the car and drove another twelve hours back to where I had just come from!

I made an agreement with myself. Once my house sale had closed, I would gift myself time to do whatever I wanted. This was my self-prescribed therapy to put a smile back on my face and in my heart. Although my heart and I were not on speaking terms, I still carried on doing what I felt was best. Whatever it took to make me happy was on the list.

Being newly single again, and thus my own boss, I was the CEO, CFO, and camp counselor of this endeavor. So, when I got back into my old town my friend, Agent 007, invited me to go scuba diving with her and her husband, I didn't think twice. I said yes! I got in their truck, and we drove down to the Florida Keys to go diving with a boat in tow. They took care of everything. I just had to sit in the back seat. I didn't realize how exhausted I truly was as I just stared out the window. I had to just be the passenger. That's all I could do anyway.

I am pretty sure my angels swooped in behind the scenes and nudged more friends to call with additional invitations. I had a surge of invites to do all sorts of fun travel trips! I said yes to almost everything! The spark of motivation to not be a hermit any longer was ignited. I put my sadness and heartbreak on hold for a bit longer in search of my smile.

The day we got back from the Keys, I dropped my tanks and scuba gear at Agent 007's house, switched suitcases, and went to the airport with another friend. We flew to Ohio and went to Kelley's Island and Cedar Point. We had a blast! Going bye-bye again was like my angels breathing some much-needed life back into me. I was handled with kid gloves at every turn. It occurred to me that I was already re-imprinting old memories as I had just been to Cedar Point the year prior!

When I got back from Ohio, it was safe for me to drive back to North Carolina as the hurricane had passed. I just beat my shipping pods' arrival with my belongings. My kids flew in to help me unload and unpack. I was so grateful for their help.

After they left, I then reloaded my dive gear and flew to Miami and met up with a large group of my dive buddies. Doing that felt like home as well! We jetted off to Bonaire for a week and it was *AH-MAZ-ING*. This trip also held some bittersweet memories, but I was insistent on re-imprinting new ones. My diving friends helped. Nothing old was ever holding me back again! I refused to shy away from a trip because of a past memory. The week trip was over, and I hugged everyone goodbye in Miami and flew to my new home in North Carolina.

Three days later, I repacked my suitcase and flew to Las Vegas with another group of friends to celebrate one of their birthdays. I even saw three Cirque du Soleil shows and came home to the positive in my piggy bank. Thank you, angels!

I admit I had barely addressed my thoughts, feelings, or battered heart since the divorce and move. I did everything I could to not think. So, I continued to say yes to everything for a few weeks, which helped. On the outside I looked fine but, on the inside, I was truly hurt, exhausted and needed to regroup. My goal was to stay in *yes* mode. To do this I knew I couldn't be still for any great length of time. If I did, I felt my heart would make me start to deal with the internal mess. I knew that I wasn't ready just yet, nor did I know how or what addressing the mess looked like.

Did I win the lottery to do, go, and see all that I did in such a short period of time? No! I did have a ton of airline points that I cashed in and used some of the proceeds from my house sale. To me, this was a celebration of my freedom and a sort of self-prescribed therapy. My angels helped set it all up. I asked for signs for every decision. I think they felt it was going to be good for me. I had become a recluse during the divorce proceedings. Because of the travel, I was a hermit no more! I am so grateful I was granted time to jet around and have fun. It was like an adult recess for me! My inner child was out and playing again.

Alas, the trips were over. I was back in North Carolina. It was just me, myself and I. My heart and soul were most certainly not agreeing on where to even begin or what to address moving forward. I loved my new place and the freedom it afforded me, but the light in my eyes and my energy had slowly diminished again. I felt withdrawn and alone since I moved away from everything I knew, but it was the best place for me to be.

Despite my stress level finally relaxing to a level it had not been in years, I was still exhausted. When people say they are tired, more often than not, it is more than physical exhaustion. It's *soul exhaustion*. I know now that was where I was at. My soul was tired. I didn't realize it though for a long time. Even if I had, I wouldn't have known what to do about it.

So, I gave myself permission to be still and only do the bare minimum for a bit as it felt safe to do so. Then I slowly started to embrace my newfound freedom. I began traveling back and forth between states for work, to see the kids and go on trips when I could. Yes, I admit I was trying to play hooky from the healing work I needed to do. Slowly, my personality and the light in my eyes started to kick back in a little more each day, becoming at last a former version of myself that I recognized when I looked in the mirror.

It hit me one morning that my recess time was coming to an end. I had to quit avoiding the elephant in the room and address the work I had to do. My healing work. I had no idea what it entailed or how to do it, but I realized I finally felt strong enough to address it. This didn't sound like fun, but I knew I needed to do it. I added this request for help to my prayers in the morning. I asked my angels to show me what I needed to do.

First on the list was continuing to rest. I had little to no obligations and the freedom to walk around in my new town where no one knew me. I was no one and I embraced that. I could wear a messy bun, no makeup, sweatpants and I didn't care. I must say, this was the first step in putting myself first. It had been years since I had no one to take care of but myself. It felt really good to do so.

After a bit more time had passed, I realized I was feeling better. Ever do one small task and think you're fixed? Yep, that was me! One and done. Was I? Nope! Not even close! I don't think we are ever fully done healing though. I came to an agreement with my angels— well, OK, I just "announced" that I was done with all this *healing stuff*, and I wanted to take a break. I am pretty sure they just laughed that I thought putting a swipe of mascara on would render me fixed and ready to venture out again.

You see, in the past, I only worked on my outside appearance after a breakup before putting myself back out into the world. I never addressed what was going on deep inside or figured out the root causes. Spirit informed me through the readings I received for myself, that this time I had to work on the inside first. This would *create a solid foundation for me going forward,* they said.

I don't really know who I am anymore. I know I need to figure that part out, too. All I know is the time I have been granted was needed in more ways than one. It gave me a chance to pause and breathe. I am done with band-aids and temporary fixes. I also don't want to be out there like I was before, either.

My angels and I have an agreement. OK, well again, I told them what I wanted. Now comes the arduous task of implementing some of what I have learned so far. Doing so means I cannot be a hermit or just sit behind my computer and write about it. Wish me luck!

Oh, and just for the record, I think I'm going to handle retirement really well!

CHAPTER 5

MESSAGES FROM BEYOND

During my divorce, I had good days and not-so-good days. I can look back now and say that if it weren't for going through that scarring experience, I probably wouldn't be where I am today. I learned a lot. So, for that, I thank him. It certainly was an experience that I will not be repeating.

At times of extremely high stress, I look for comfort in the smallest of things. It could be a call from a friend, a hug, or a situation you thought would be worse that ended up being easy. It's moments of gratefulness in the littlest of things that steady my life. They keep me grounded when my world is being flipped upside down, turned inside out, and spun out of control.

When a ballerina does a pirouette, they are taught to "spot," or affix, their gaze on something steady and unmoving so they don't get dizzy. My great-aunt Arline became and still is, my focus spot.

My great-aunt passed away when I was in my early twenties. She and I share the same birthday. I remember visiting her a few times when I was younger, before she passed. I own her baby shoes now (she was born in 1926), her roller skates with wooden wheels from when she was a teenager, and her address book from when she was an adult. I have since seen home movies this past year of her and could see such a similarity in our demeanors. When people ask, "If you could bring someone back from heaven who would it be?" I'd pick her. My great-aunt Arline's trademark had been drawing a smiling face with ears after she wrote something. I also do that but without the ears.

There are many a time when lights flicker in my house. I am not talking a blink on or off. I am talking about it appearing as Morse code or something! My kids used to joke about it. It didn't happen all the time or with any consistency or regularity to be able to say it was an electrical problem. I will tell you that after the verticals moving incident, I paid attention to everything!

Years ago, before I moved to North Carolina, the house I moved from had sliding glass doors out to a lanai with verticals on them. One night I was sitting on my couch watching a late-night show on TV. I had been sitting there for a while and noticed that two of the verticals closer to the end were moving in tandem. I honestly didn't think anything of it. Maybe the AC was on and blew them? I sat there for a while, still watching them. They were still moving. They did not stop. Again, it was only two of the vertical veins, right next to each other.

Without moving off the couch, I timed their strange movements. In fact, I had not moved at all! I was a good sixteen feet away. I looked at the clock. The same steady, methodical movement was repeating. It was like a metronome. Not faster, nor slower. I finally got up and looked at the thermostat. It was completely off. I was now another twelve feet further away and they did not slow or change pace. I took a picture of the thermostat to prove it was off. I took a picture of the ceiling fan to prove it was off. I even went to the opposite side of the sliding doors and looked at the glass. The slider was closed and locked. The two swinging panels were at the opposite end. The movement of the other end of the slider did not change anything either. Me walking (the only air movement) did not change the cadence at which they swung. At one point, thoughts of my great-aunt popped into my head. This was a very random thought to have. Could it be her? Could she be doing this? To me, the rhythmic movement reminded me of a person sitting on a ledge, swinging their legs back and forth. I was not scared! There were no odd feelings that would cause me concern. So, I videotaped it, showing it with a time and date stamp provided by the TV. I wanted proof to show my kids the next day. It just kept moving and didn't stop. Finally, it was time for me to go to bed. I went to my room and closed my door.

The next morning when I got up, I slowly opened up my door to look into the living room and the exact two veins of mini blinds were still moving at the same speed! I took my phone, stuck my hand out the bedroom door and videotaped it again. I did not know who or what was going on.

I moved freely through the house just eyeing the blinds to see if their movement would change and it didn't.

I had to leave the house to run some errands. When I came back, they were *still* moving. If I remember correctly, it ended up being around eighteen hours straight. I knew a spirit was in there doing it. I had it on video!

I didn't know who it was, nor did I know how to ask. It wasn't until I began seeing my birthdate on the clock—a *lot*. Since the time of the blind movement, I would coincidentally see the time. Seriously, day and night. I could open a book, see my birthday as the page number, see a license plate with the number, see it on paperwork, and hear it on TV. Everywhere I looked, for about a week or so after, I kept seeing the repeated number so much that I felt the need to bring it up to others for their thoughts. The question in my mind was, why? Why was my birthday showing up so much and why did I keep seeing it? This was my introduction to number signs.

I don't know the exact moment it hit me, but I had gone to a local reader who was a saint in providing guidance from the other side during my divorce. My great-aunt Arline had come through, along with my grandfather (her brother), and that is when I put two and two together. *My great-aunt was trying to talk to me*! She was showing me our birthday numbers to identify herself. That is why she popped into my head at first when I saw the blinds moving. I felt such comfort that she had found a way to make it known that it was her and my grandfather there. Now, I get it.

Since knowing that it was my great-aunt, I must give credit for the effort she (and my grandfather) put in to help me (and still do!) from the other side. The sheer coincidence of how many times, when I was falling apart in private during my divorce, someone from my core group of friends would call or text to see how I was doing was amazing! It was like my great-aunt and grandfather knew I needed help and sent my friends a nudge to reach out. I know it was them.

On one of the many days that I felt frustrated during my divorce, I was trying to multitask, doing work on the computer through tears. It was at that time that I looked at the computer screen and actually saw the advertisement on the right. It felt as if a hand was on either side of my face that gently moved my head in the direction of my computer to look. When I finally saw what it was, I could only stare. There was a big yellow smiling face and the ad said, "*We Got You, Honey!*"

Through my tears, I just stared in awe. I did not have to think twice about it. I just knew it was my great-aunt reaching through in a manner she could put into words, along with her trademark, what she wanted me to know. She and my grandfather had my back! I wish I had taken a picture of it. I had never seen this ad before on the computer. I swear I stared at that for at least five minutes—literally just stared. As I did, those words were tucked into my heart as hope where I had felt none. I kept those words: *We Got You, Honey!* handwritten on my desk blotter for the remainder of my divorce as a reminder that there was something much bigger in play.

The spirits had a plan in place to hold my hand through the fire and help me out. They did just that.

CHAPTER 6

TUG-OF-WAR: ME VS. ANGELS

Once upon a time, I was under the illusion I was in control. Then, reality came and slapped me in the face. I learned that things did not go my way all the time. *GASP*! Frankly, this little nuance kind of irritated me. Seriously, I did everything I felt was right, and yet, what I wanted didn't happen. I was blind to the "whys."

I look back at events in my life and how they come back full circle. So, I had this little game that I played. If I did not win, I wasn't going to play. That was going to be the guarantee. Maybe it was intuition that told me I would succeed. If it was, I had no idea. I suspect as I fumbled my way around in our formative years, that I was the source of great laughter to my angels and loved ones, as I tried to run when I barely had learned to crawl. I did not care who my opponent was. No matter what, if I did not think or know I would win, I just did not play. You cannot lose if you do not play, right? WINNER WINNER, CHICKEN DINNER! So, in a way, that was my own security blanket of my, imagined, control. I took myself out of the game if I wasn't going to win.

As a child, I wanted so desperately to do something like sleep over at Stacy or Kelly's house. I knew darn well how many months I literally had to bribe my stepfather for even a chance to be able to. If I couldn't, I said out loud in prayer, "There is a reason why, and I trust you."

Fast forward to all sorts of lessons, upside down and backward, as I am in the beginning throes of the "adulting" arena. This was a little bit more challenging. Being around more adults and also in real estate, I now felt the need to study and learn the nuances of everyone around me. It was a need to understand what their tactics and motives were. There were people more skilled in getting what they wanted. I felt the need to ramp up my understanding so I could learn. To me it was like a game of chess, so to speak. I had to contemplate their moves to make my move. It was just my way of fitting myself into different experiences and hoping for the best.

As I was now "adulting" more and more, I was also becoming intrigued by spiritual stuff. Along with that came a few phrases that I did not like. They didn't fit in with my master plan! Phrases like "let go," "just believe," and "have faith." Uh, that's a big *no*. Let's just keep doing things my way! If you haven't noticed, I can be quite stubborn—after all, if you aren't going to let me win and I know it, I'm not going to play. (Hey, it was working so far!)

Well, life has a way of making you play. It's kind of like the movie *Jumanji*—you must roll the dice to be dealt your next task or you're stuck dealing with whatever you got. It's not anything like the board game Life, where you have the car with pink and blue pegs in it and easily get to the end. Life is just one task, lesson, and journey after another that you must figure out.

In my career, I had tried to be everything to everyone while perfecting my people-pleasing skills. Doing so meant I had a plan. Now, if everyone just did what I wanted, it would work! I had held on so tightly to this notion that, I swear, if the notion was a rock, I would have been in *The Guinness Book of World Records* as the first woman to squeeze blood out of it. Yep! I held on that tightly.

Of course, with the ongoing battle of wills between myself and the angels if I didn't see myself winning, I just dropped it. I usually had exhausted myself by then. I finally would just say, "Let the chips fall where they may." Mind you, I may or may not have also said a lovely four-letter word that begins with F and then ended it with IT. You get the picture.

What I learned that just shocked my knickers off, was when I let go of what I was holding on to so tightly it fell into place by itself. Was it like I thought it should be? Nope! Nonetheless, it worked out. That made me curious, how the hell did that happen? How come I didn't see things falling into place that way? Could those long, drawn-out events have been fixed sooner if I had just let go?

Am I good at letting it all go? That's a big fat *no*! I am the captain of my ship, in charge of steering through waters. If I am steering, I know I am going to make it, right? Well, that is how it's supposed to happen in my storybook.

I kept trying to do it my way. But I noticed the more I held on, the more I became exhausted and frankly did not care. If you are around me when I'm in that state, you will enter the wrath of cold. I will block you out of my life in any way that I see fit and not respond to you in any way, shape or form. Humor me. It's my inner child feeling like she's doing something.

It was starting to feel like I was playing a game of tug-of-war with my angels and guardians. I used to win all the time but now, it was not working. I would use all of my strength and willpower to make something happen. So, why not, now? Fast forward to one of many "heart-to-hearts" while praying. Let's just say, since they were not going to let me win at everything, I could see there was a lesson to learn instead. I don't like learning lessons.

Backtracking to the final chapters of my divorce. I had sought counsel at a few metaphysical shops and learned bits and pieces along the way in my journey. One of the big things that I learned is that life on earth is like school for us. If you don't do your work and learn the lessons, I believe you have to come back to earth and do it again. Well, I don't know about you, but that fear was pretty big for me.

For years and years while dating, I repeatedly did not learn my lesson. I kept thinking if I tried harder, gave more, loved more, expected less, and so on that it would be better the next time. I knew we had a soul connection and felt we were supposed to be together. Alas, his patterns and habits repeated like clockwork and gave me cause to walk away. I was hurt over and over. I spent hours trying to figure out what I did wrong this time. When I felt better, I fluffed up the outside, and jumped back into the relationship again. This pattern continued after we were married. No matter what I did, it still didn't work. That's when I finally hit the wall and went to see my attorney.

I will never forget his advice the first time I visited him six months after we were married. He told me that *I wasn't ready to leave.* He said I would be wasting money because he didn't hear the resolve to be done. Can you imagine that? An attorney turned me away because I wasn't ready.

Anyway, I would get breadcrumbs of good behavior for a second and then the questionable behavior got worse. I knew that I was really done when I was crying under water while scuba diving! For real! I cried. In my world, it got that bad. If the fish had tissues, they would have offered some to me. My heart was screaming for me to let this go. Have faith—*blind faith*—that I would be all right if I did. I needed to let go of this heavy rock that was drowning me. I was exhausted, and I just wanted out. I was ready to let the chips fall where they may. The struggle was real. I did not want to hold on to it anymore.

One morning soon thereafter, I could not sleep. I had this routine of going out to the end of my driveway and just sitting there praying. I adore the stars and the moon, and I feel so at home when I'm outside. When I pray, I talk out loud and speak as if my angels are literally right in front of me. My neighbors walking their dogs before work thought I was squirrely, but I did not care. It is very therapeutic for me to speak out loud. It was at that moment that I finally let go of the rock. Through tears, I said, *"I am done. I don't ever want to feel like this again. I will not come back to earth and do this shit ever again. I will walk through whatever fire you need me to. I am that done. Get me out. I SURRENDER."*

And then, I let it go.

There was a peace that came over me that I can't explain. It was to that point that the fear of staying the same was greater than the fear of change. I have since learned that is the catalyst for me. When the fear of staying the same is greater than the fear of change, that is when I seem to hold my nose and jump into action. I know I probably make it way more difficult on myself than I need to at times. Regardless, it's my way of doing things.

After that extremely profound moment, I jumped into action. It was now one year after we got married and I was done—wanted out, badly. I was directed by nudges that helped me do what I needed to do. My ex even said something seemed different about me. My energy had shifted, and he could probably sense this.

Now remember, I told my angels I was willing to walk through fire and fire it was. The divorce was no cakewalk. It hurt. I was under pressure. I got burned, and they got me out. There is a saying that rings true for me: the only way out is through.

One Sunday, I took a drive out to an island to clear my head. The sunroof and windows were open, and I flipped through radio stations and came across a Joel Osteen sermon that caught my attention. It was about a piece of coal turning into a diamond by being under pressure. Something about that clicked. I felt like I did, indeed, go through fire, but I was now a diamond. I felt like I had new facets, and my eyes were starting to slowly shine again. I was now a diamond and hands down; I had angels on my side.

Having learned some big lessons already, do I blindly let go of everything? (Cough-cough) Sure I do! Not! If I do feel like I am holding on too tightly, the memory of me at the end of my driveway making that agreement pops up in my head. It reminds me to try and release my hold. Many times, it is not as easy as it sounds.

Meanwhile, because I am in a good place, I wrote myself a pep talk letter while I was in a great mood. It's labeled ICE (In Case of Emergency) Yes, it's to me, from me. I have reminders of things I might be blind to if I decide to put rose-colored glasses back on or be swayed to opt in again. It is a reminder of what I need to do to pull my bootstraps up and move forward. It's in a sealed envelope, just in case.

I have learned a lot in the past few years. If I am going to have to walk through fire again, I am putting on my mirrored aviator sunglasses, folding my ICE letter and putting it in my back pocket.

Then I am grabbing a stick and a bag of marshmallows to roast!

CHAPTER 7

SPIRIT JUNKIE

When I first started on this journey, there were little bits and pieces that came at me, and it was like catching hearts in the wind. I was excited and yet there was so much to learn and more that I wanted to know.

There is and has been a fine line between those you speak to about spiritual stuff. Some make it sound perfectly normal to have a spiritual side and want to do things with it, while others roll their eyes. If this helps me that's all I care about. Roll those eyes! I just hope they don't get dizzy.

Frankly, I was seriously excited and didn't know where to start or what to do first. I have been told for many, many years that I am a medium. Who, me? Not sure where they got that from, but ... OK! I was not ready for that.

I began by signing up for Meet Up groups in North Carolina. I looked under the spiritual and metaphysical categories at the options that were available. The first one I signed up for was mediumship. I had no idea what I was supposed to do so I was hoping they would teach me how.

In the first class I went to, it was obvious that it was an ongoing class, and I came in the middle of it. So, no lie, the teacher just announced off the bat, "We are going to stand up one at a time and give a reading." *GULP* What the hell? I sat there in awe and wonder. Was it that easy? How did I know? Who was it? Um, teacher, I am not ready to talk to dead people! I don't know what I am doing. When do you teach me what to do?

When it was my turn, I followed suit like the others, stood up and whatever came to mind I said. This made the girl I was talking to start crying! Jeez, Louise! I don't know where what I said came from. I said to that girl I was sorry! OK, maybe this mediumship wasn't for me. I did not know what I was doing, and this wasn't a teaching class.

I decided to back off on anything that had to do with mediumship. Making people cry was not the best way to make friends in a new town! I looked online again and opted for a different course. This one was on pictometry.

The assignment was for everyone to bring a picture of a deceased loved one, put it in a sealed envelope, and then we passed the envelopes around. When it was your turn you held a random envelope, then wrote your impressions down on the back of it, then passed it to the next person. The owner of the picture then would read off the impressions and give any validation.

What I did notice is that although I couldn't tell you about the people in the picture, I was getting images of other things in the picture around the people! I was plumb-proud of myself. This stuff might be right up my alley!

The bigger question I was asking myself, was why I did not want to receive any information about the deceased person in the picture. I realized allowing connection to the people in the pictures scared me. I had to think about why.

A memory popped into my head of a psychic medium I had met with a few years prior. When I asked him how he got started, he told me his story. Part of it was of him taking a shower. He had turned around and felt a spirit with him that wanted him to relay a message. He had to get stern with that spirit and say, "Do NOT frighten me!"

He explained that when you are "open" to receive, you get everyone and anyone. You have to set boundaries. (UGH! That "b" word!) He told the "other side" that certain times he was off limits. One very specific time was when he closed his bedroom door. No one was allowed in there with him.

Well let me tell you, the conversation with him brought up a *lot* more questions! So, spirits see what goes on in your bedroom and what you're doing? Um, oh-my-goodness. Wait, can they see everything? (I kept thinking of my great-aunt and grandparents! Oh, if this is true, they must be rolling over in their graves!) So, if you forget to set the boundary, do spirits just hang around you like a stalker ghost? I had so many more questions! I didn't want a stage-five clinger spirit!

After I left that session, I just point-blank said, *"If you all scare me, I am not doing this! Got it? Capeesh?"* There were plenty of times after finding this out, I even said, "No one gets to come in the bedroom!"

Just in case you're wondering what they can and can't see, I am told you aren't "seen" in the physical but more on an energetic level. Still, I can't fathom my grandparents and great-aunt in the room. No, no, and *hell* no! Hard pass!

I recalled visiting with another reader who felt something touched her elbow during my reading and she randomly yelled out, "*no touchy*!" I just looked at her. I could not see anything, but she said, while rubbing her elbow, that her hard boundaries are no physical touch. Something touched her and she felt it. Hmmm. That's when it got very interesting to me.

I think having heard and seen these instances gave me a sort of mental block to mediumship and frankly scared me a bit. So pictometry was sort of a way around it all.

Anyway, I searched for books on the subject. I realized that everyone has their own experiences and nuances, so there is not one catch-all-be-all about any of this. There is no official handbook.

I started with the book *Opening to Channel*, which spoke of meditating, UGH! The bane of my existence was front and center. I had to learn to quiet my mind. That meant I had to deal with all the hamster wheels and soapboxes in there. Talk about overwhelming!

I gave myself five minutes. I sat in the grass, put the timer on my phone, and told my brain, OK, be quiet for just five minutes! I'm not going to lie; meditating took more than a few tries. I finally got to five minutes. I thought about when I was a child having to go to bed despite the sun still being up, and I used to say, "Dark, black room." I would visualize with my eyes closed, a room with just a single chair in the middle and no sun could come in this room—thus waking me up. I would just say that over and over again like a chant and eventually, I'd fall asleep. I figured this was the same thing really, just the "adult version."

I would eventually graduate to fifteen minutes of meditation. Then, pictures started popping into my head. When it got to more than three pictures, I felt the need to write them down. I practiced writing with my eyes closed. Something was finally happening, and it was cool!

I then found Sonia Choquette's books. I listened to the audiobook version and liked the content and her voice. It was about the angels and spirit guides who exist around everyone. I then graduated to books about signs, and how messages might look to you and ways to interpret them.

Frankly, it spiraled from there. The more I worked on and learned about this stuff, the more elated I was. I can't tell you how important it was to know others who didn't think of me as possessed! This was such cool stuff!

I stumbled across a YouTube tarot card reader, and it was like she knew exactly what was going on with me even though she had never met me!

I had a tarot deck of my own but reading for yourself is very biased. You could look a meaning up on the computer and just pick the one you liked the best that fit your heart's desire. I resonated with a few tarot card layout books and their meaning and purchased them.

I will tell you what, when the student is ready, the teacher will appear. Not everyone has days upon days to study, read, and practice.

Having moved to a new place, all I had was time. I was in a new town, with no household responsibilities, no kids in tow because they were on their own and was not traveling as much. This time allowed me to really get the hang of this stuff.

I then found the Rhine (Rhine.org) by Duke University and they had a group called PEG (Psychic Exchange group), a DREAM group, and a REMOTE VIEWING group. I also stumbled across some classes at metaphysical stores in the area. I was *hooked*, I tell ya! All of this just made sense to me—sense in a way that nothing else really did. I did not need to talk myself into anything. The desire was simply natural.

It was like an adrenaline rush. Suddenly, everything in my midst was magical. I would call upon guides to find me parking spots; I would ask questions and give signs for answers and get them. Electrical occurrences and knocks were no longer "spooky or eerie," they were my friends! The stuff that happened as I was growing up made *mountains* of sense, finally, too. It made sense to me as to why I liked the things I did, why some things didn't scare me but were fascinating. From then on, it was a feast of books, courses, crystals, notes galore and practice. I was captivated to say the least!

It is fun and hands down magical when you realize that occurrences in your life that you can't explain are not made up! They are not only real but also have an explanation to boot! I just wanted to learn more!

The little bubble of existence I created to learn and grow felt safe. Safe to speak and just be while I was in North Carolina. When I traveled back home though, I put back on my other identities— mom, friend, and coworker. I had to shut down this part of me to the people who were not open to it. Frankly, it felt weird. Like, I would have thought that getting into the metaphysics would be the weird part, but it was actually reverting back to who I was before. That is what felt odd to me.

So, I live a double life. I want to know, learn, do, see and speak openly if asked about metaphysics. I feel that I have graduated to a higher level of learning and still have lots to go, though. Putting on my game face for family and friends and then lighting up when I can talk freely and discuss the cool experiences with other like-minded friends is enchanting.

When you realize you have ways to know the inside scoop on what is going on in your life and that of others, you can't help but be excited. There are so many things to still know to progress to a higher level of learning!

It's a fine line when your worlds bleed together, and you have a choice to embrace who you have become and grow away from who you used to be. Having support from both sides is paramount. Figuring out how to blend the two worlds continues to be a challenge I can't wrap my head around yet, but I am learning.

CHAPTER 8

OWNING "IT"

I can do things. Metaphysical talents. Not just one, but many. I am not perfect at any one thing, but a student of them all. Describing me as "fascinated" with what I have learned so far is an understatement!

Before I get into my cool-ass experiences thus far, I am going to be honest here and admit a struggle of mine. *AHEM* (drum roll please!) I have a problem owning in public what I can do. In private, no problem. Public though? Not-so-much!

Trust me, I make no apologies about what I can do and what I'm learning. It's *talking* about my abilities that I have problem with. At what point do you bring it up? Do I have to? Nope! I just think some of the key fundamental people in your world should know. There are only a small handful of people, I will admit, that I truly do care if they know or not. Some would think it would be so easy to just say it and get it over with! For me, it's just not that easy.

So, let's just break this down into what it really is about for me, shall we?

Fear.

There, I said it. I am human and want to belong and feel accepted. What I run the risk of is exactly what most people crave, yet fear. Standing out. Rejection and criticism are a few of the massive verbal slugs one can give another. I want to point out that fear is a two-way street. If you fear something, it is because you don't understand, accept, or approve of it. To justify this fear, you may try to make someone else feel bad about their choices or ideas, hoping that they will change to make *you* feel better. In a nutshell, I have a fear of telling people about my abilities, and some of those people have a fear of the unknown.

What the hell is my problem then? You know, I don't know. If I didn't believe it, I wouldn't speak it. To give you an example, let me tell you about Stan.

I have an old friend from school, Stan. I have always had an affinity for him—there's something about him I gravitate to. In my eyes, he and his family are just wonderful people. Over the years, Stan's mom, dad, and brother have all passed. I knew his mom the best but also his brother for a brief few years before he died.

They both randomly came to me in my meditation and said that when I was ready, they would like me to give Stan and his family a message from them. (Truly, I would be honored!)

I called Stan to chat and catch up for a few. Stan even commented on our connection as just a handful of everlasting good souls that can pick up the phone and talk to like no time has passed! I then told him of the messages that I had for him. I explained my pending trip overseas to learn and develop skills to do this more effectively. Then, I asked if he would be open to hearing more when I was more prepared? (Trust me, I held my breath.) He said yes.

He was kind to me. He asked how I knew if it was them or someone else. He did tell me that he did believe enough and that he and his wife watch a few metaphysical shows on TV. I thanked him, and we hung up the phone. That is when the panic set in.

I will be honest and say that it bothered me a *lot*. What did he think? Was he just being nice? Was he gossiping about me? I went off the deep end thinking of a bunch of scenarios that could happen and who he might tell. Would my secret come out now? I had to let it go and resolve the fact that if I didn't believe it myself, I would *not* have put myself at risk to mention it.

Did that make me feel better? Well, it did after it set in about a week later. Spirit worked really hard to calm my butt down over this by putting like-minded friends in my path to console me and let me get the panic out of my system.

Stan was relatively easy to communicate with as I was not only in another state but on the phone. (Got to love hiding behind a phone!) But next on the list to speak to about this were the big three in my life. Those three who are not so amenable are the ones who are closest to me: my two sons and my mom.

You would think they would be the easy ones, right? Nope! Seriously, for me it would be much easier to walk up to a stranger or stand in front of a crowd of people and say, "I have spiritual gifts," than to tell my kids and my mom. I think it is due to not knowing if they would support my beliefs or not. I have always kept my thoughts and ideas neutral and noncommittal before. Saying something would be a very bold statement for me.

I am going to next week though. Well, say something at least. I want to explain that I am flying overseas to "Hogwarts" for training.

I mentioned it to my mom briefly in conversation today and all she said was, "Oh."

At the local Mind Body & Spirit Expo I had attended in Raleigh; I received some good advice from a local metaphysical practitioner. I explained my plight about telling my family, and as a fellow parent he said, "*Your kids (or anyone, for that matter) don't get to dictate what you like or don't like. Nor do they get to tell YOU what to do with YOUR life. It's up to them to figure out what to do with the information you give them. Tell them what the deal is and let them figure out the best way to explain or not explain what you are doing.*"

That was some of the best life advice I have received in a long time! Now to just apply it!

CHAPTER 9

HOW DO YOUR SPOONS BEND?

I feel like a sponge. I seem to be constantly searching to see what else there is to learn and what I can do! Duke University has a group called The Rhine (www.Rhine.org) that J. B. Rhine founded many years ago to explore metaphysical events. Of course, I had to go and check it out.

I felt like I found a collective of people who also shared similar events and occurrences. It is an open forum—a safe space—to speak of your experiences without judgment. Upon attending the meetings, I heard many stories of different ways that spirits get your attention to give you messages. This was fascinating!

I got wind they were hosting ESP Games, so I signed up. I just wanted to know if and what I could do in addition to what I already knew! There were about twenty-five of us in attendance for the evening.

We were divided into three groups for particular events. The first group event was Zener Cards, which started with five different images on nontransparent paper. The reader shuffled the cards and held up each one. The rest of us had a pencil and paper and we were to use our minds to "see" what the card was and mark it down. If I remember correctly, I got a modest score, but nothing significant. The lady across from me, though, got twenty-two out of twenty-five!

The next "test" was to hold a closed orange envelope and talk about the picture inside. One person was more specific than the rest of us but there were about four to five of us that all claimed the same items in a picture. We couldn't open the rest of the envelopes to validate what we saw in our mind's eye. I got a few shapes consistent with the picture but nothing to write home about!

The next battery of tests was to see if we had "predictive" abilities. There were four stations to try. We were to predict how the pattern of lights, sounds or objects would show up. I scored the highest out of our cluster of the twenty-five people in the group.

There were a few other tests that we were able to try, which were a lot of fun to see how far our individual abilities extended!

At the end of the evening, we all gathered once again into one room. The final event of the evening was to practice spoon bending. This seemed like it was going to be fun! I had no clue how to do it, but they gave us instructions. Basically, you use your mind's energy to command the spoon to bend, then divert your attention for a moment, then come back to the spoon and it will bend easily. It took about four different spoons, but once I got the hang of it, *it bent so easily*! No tools.

Oh my gosh, I was so excited I could do this! They allowed us to keep the spoons, too! There are actual documented cases where a person can make the spoon bend by thought alone. I was just happy with my accomplishment to make it easily curl.

I was so happy that I attended this event. I left that night having won my very own GOT ESP coffee mug for having the highest score in one of the events. It was such a cool evening!

CHAPTER 10

SIMPLE SIGNS

Flying by the seat of my pants this year, I have been open to go, do, and see just about anything that I feel like doing. Some of it has been for work when necessary but most of it was for pleasure. So, when my good friend called me from Blue Ridge, Georgia, and asked me to come hang out. The answer was yes! Have car: will travel. Blue Ridge holds a lot of special memories for me and is an old stomping ground.

Before I went, I asked my friend if she would be open to me giving her a channeled reading from spirit while there. I was pretty new at it still and needed practice. She was very open to it. So again, knowing a lot about her, I prefaced our meeting to not tell me anything at all prior to my arrival as to not influence what might come through.

I threw my stuff in the car and went. It was a glorious drive through mountains, seeing once again places I had been before. Once there at the cabin she rented, we kept the chitchat to surface conversations, and just enjoyed the scenery.

Finally, we sat down to do the reading. Right now, I channel spirit with my eyes closed. I do not want to be influenced by body language or reactions to anything that I may or may not say. I went through my routine to start, and then all sorts of information came out. When I was done, I asked her for any validation she could give me.

We both agreed that since I know her, some of the things mentioned could be because of my awareness of her and her life events. Then, there were the things I had no clue about.

For example, spirit mentioned her nephew. She explained to me the strife he was experiencing at the moment. I know her nephew but had no way of knowing that information as I had extracted myself from all social media after the divorce and had not since restarted it. That was further validation to me.

Part of my present routine after a reading is to have the sitter shuffle a deck of Angel Oracle Cards and pick a few. So, she shuffled, putting her own energy onto the deck by touching it, and drew three cards. The cards validated the messages that spirit told her through me.

She looked at each individual card and their message and said, "OH! You told me this!" This happened with all three cards she picked. Feeling that maybe the deck was possibly rigged, she asked to see the rest of the deck. I handed it to her, respecting her desire to see and validate for herself. After verbally confirming that a good many of the cards did not apply to her, she took the cards she chose as being meant for her.

The visit was relaxing and fun and we had many laughs and fantastic conversations. One afternoon during one of our talks, we sat in the living room of the cabin on opposite couches. We noticed that the thermostat light kept coming on. Was it motion-activated? No one was moving. We had been sitting and talking for at least thirty to forty minutes at that time. The air wasn't on. The fan wasn't on. We weren't and hadn't been moving.

Suddenly, the picture on the wall in the open stairwell behind my friend fell off the wall. Let me tell you that my friend jumped! I just looked and felt unphased. The picture was held by two nails on the wall. Somehow, I knew it was someone in spirit with us, making themselves known.

Another thing that happened while we were all playing games one evening was the light over the dining table, which was super dim, suddenly grew significantly brighter. My friend and her son were shocked because they had tried and couldn't figure out how to get it to go brighter, yet it did by itself. They told me that the day before they even tried to replace the light bulbs but couldn't figure it out. We were all in awe!

The screened porch overlooking the mountains was inviting and amazing. The owners had a string of lights that zigzagged across the patio. On my last day, I got up early to watch the sunrise and say my prayers when the lights suddenly came on. I told my friend that it was a nice touch that the lights were on a motion detector. She vehemently insisted that they were not on a motion detector but, in fact, on a remote that was in her purse inside the house.

I just smiled. To me, that further validated that there were spirits around.

CHAPTER 11

SYMBOLS: THE OVER-THE-SHOULDER BOULDER HOLDER

As I have progressed in my journey, the subject of symbols and meanings has come up quite a bit. When I first started meditating, I saw pictures in my mind but had no idea what they meant. This led me on a journey to figure it out. The first thing I did was order a book on symbols. It was by another medium who took the time to explain what exactly her signs and symbols were and what they looked like. I read it cover to cover. As I was reading all the things she wrote out, the thought of memorizing her meanings of signs seemed daunting, so I put the book away.

As I continued to meditate, I saw things like rosary beads, a coffin, a sleeping lion, and other weird but distinctive signs. I started a notebook to write down what came to me. I wrote the words of some pictures that seemed obvious and drew out what I could see in my mind, but not yet explain. I noticed that along with my pictures and words, there was most likely a message that went along with those pictures. I had no clue what the messages were about. I knew that what I was receiving meant something but how to tie it together eluded me. I just kept writing and drawing. This stuff was fascinating! Of course, at times I patted myself on the back for having a fantastic imagination, but if I had control of my imagination, would I not be in control of the content I imagined?

As I attended more classes, the drive to "create your own symbols book" came up with more frequency. It was like a buzz-phrase for me that stood out. What finally occurred to me is that what you think something means and what I think something means could be very different. For example, to some, a sleeping lion could mean, literally, that a lion is sleeping. It could also be a symbol of someone powerful not looking because their eyes were closed. It might also mean that, although sleeping and looking docile, once they wake up and are aware, someone will once again be fierce and strong. Possibly the representation of the sleeping lion is a metaphor for someone who is going to be waking up into a strong and powerful leader.

I learned recently that everyone's perception is colored by what is going on in their life as well as personal experiences. It doesn't make anyone right or wrong. It did make it necessary for me to come up with my own list of people, places, things, and objects. But, how? I had no clue. Pictures were coming faster the more I meditated.

There were pictures of things I drew but I had absolutely no idea what they even were! Some of them looked like symbols or markings of some ancient era. So, on a nudge while out one afternoon, I suddenly went to a Barnes and Noble. Seriously, it wasn't planned but it was like someone shouted to me, "Pull in now!" I walked into the breezeway and to the right was a display of books on gardening and to the left a display on history. Normally I just walk past them, but my eyes diverted to a single book at eye level on the end. One lone book on "symbols." It had no correlation to the subjects on display. It was the only book on the topic in the section. It was on sale. It was mine. That is most certainly an example of how spirits can move you into a place for whatever they need. I took a picture of the display to tell my friend how this transpired.

This book was (and is) simply fascinating to me. It has ancient languages, Hebrew and Latin symbols, numbers, and signs. I knew it was for me to use to decipher what these strange pictures I was drawing meant. I think the best part was that there were pictures to compare my crude drawings against. I found out a lot of things and others made no sense. I just felt like I was on the right path. Not necessarily making sense of, or if there even were any messages, but I was thoroughly entertained to see what I drew and what it meant.

As with spirits sometimes, when there is a strong push for me to do something, they align things for me that are so obvious, I just know.

I knew that my task at hand was to create my own symbols book. I investigated YouTube videos for any "how to" ideas, when I stumbled on a woman showing how she created a book to define your own symbols. It had a word and a line after so I could describe what it meant for me. The best part was that it was organized by different subjects, and it had an index. SOLD! Seriously, just by her mentioning how it was organized and indexed made me realize that my rudimentary attempts would have been a rat's nest of disorganization at the least!

The book arrived a few days later. Now, I had to fill it out. UGH. I think it was around 287 pages. I made it my mission to go to the park and fill out twenty pages, every time I went. That was my homework. Twenty pages. I had received a message to do it in pencil as my description and thoughts could change. (I thought that was a brilliant idea!) It was further revealed to me by my guides, that spirits on the other side needed to learn my language. I needed to know how they would speak through me to pass on messages for them when I was ready. OK! Fair enough!

Do you know how hard it is to put in writing all the pictures I could see and work with? Let me tell you, it's not easy. Not impossible, just very tedious! For example, if a spirit on the other side wanted to show me a lunch box, I had to think about how they needed to show it to me. I had decisions to make about this. Was it a brown box with lunch in it? Is it my Mickey Mouse lunch box with the red handle that I had when I was five? Or is it a box of food from KFC that I order at the drive-thru? Spirit needed to know, and I was supposed to tell them. This was needed so I could help them help me with readings.

I was in rare form, sitting at the park doing my homework one afternoon, rather slap-happy actually, and I came across the word "BRA" to describe. This was a moment when I could not help but channel my inner five-year-old and giggled at all the things I could write. Are there political correctness rules on the other side that I need to abide by? I decided to find out. I wrote in my symbols book under BRA: *an over-the-shoulder boulder holder (also) a torturous device created to prevent men and woman from staring at your chesticles.*

A few days later in my meditation, the message came through that they were happy about my efforts in filling out the symbols book and many were having a good laugh at my description of a bra, on the other side. I was not asked to change it! My description remains! I was happy I could make them laugh!

I owe a huge shout-out to my friends who helped me describe some of the words I struggled to interpret! It wasn't easy!

CHAPTER 12

STACY: FINDING WHAT WAS LOST!

I have a friend who I will call Stacy. Stacy and I have a longstanding friendship and have been a source of support for each other off and on since we first met. It's one of those friendships where you could just tell the hard, raw truth and get away with it. No judgment. We all need a few friends with whom we have a blanket permission slip of sorts to say whatever we need to without judgment. She is one of a handful of friends of mine that I would take criticism from.

Back in my old town for a few days, Stacy asked for a channeled reading. The fact that we both know so much about each other makes it difficult to differentiate what I already know versus what channeled messages are from spirit. So, I asked her to not tell me anything for a month and let's see what comes through.

I went to her house and read for her. There were quite a few things that were said, but I don't remember as I was in a trancelike state. She took notes and mentioned quite a few validations of things I was not privy to at that point. One thing that stood out to me was seeing where her boyfriend lived.

I described the outside of the house but most importantly, that there was a vacant lot to the left and I saw a white vehicle. Part of my message to her was that something was lost on the left side of the property.

When we were done, I asked her for any validation of the messages that came through and she said a few things to me. One of them was about what was lost. She said that her boyfriend had allowed an employee of his to live in a spare residence on his land. They happened to have a drug problem and broke into his personal property looking for some things to sell. Some items were missing. One was a gun, and one was a ring belonging to his grandmother who had passed away. I mentioned that maybe she could have her son go around the property on the left with a metal detector and see if he could find whatever was missing.

A few days later, Stacy called me and told me that they went over the left side of the property. They not only found the gun, but the *ring* and they called the police to come and fingerprint the items. I was beyond happy! That to me was significant! Stacy was so excited, she had to call me right away, but she also let me know that another friend of hers wanted a reading as well. I was in awe!

CHAPTER 13

PSST! WANT TO KNOW A SECRET?

I am now channeling spirit a lot. I have graduated to the next level in my opinion. I am not perfect yet, just no longer a beginner. I am learning all sorts of things. Frankly, it's pretty darn cool!

I just want to point out that the words and phrases that come through me are mostly not my language. I have spoken words I have literally had to look up to know what they meant, let alone spell correctly! A couple of examples would be *juxtaposed* and *double entendre*. These are not common words I use in my vocabulary. I continue to not only be amazed by some of the words but also that they are used correctly in the statement given to me. It's been rather fun doing this, I might add.

When I first got to this point, I was writing every word they said, one by one. I closed my eyes, so I was using my fingernails to hold my pen against until the next word came through. Let me tell you, I have messed up many a manicure doing it this way. A few friends told me I should just get a mini-recorder, speak out loud, and then write it down after. So, OK! I do that now and it works. I am still handwriting what they tell me in a notebook. To date, I'm now on book three, thank-you-very-much. I will graduate to typing eventually, as a friend of mine has, but I am not there yet.

Being a channel for spirits is like being at the adult dinner table. You hear all the good stuff! That being said, I feel like I have become privy to a few secrets along the way, some good, and some not so good.

First of all, I have no idea what they are going to tell through me. I just talk, and don't remember when I am done. Ever talk to a friend and they say, "That was really good! Can you say that again?" and then not remember anything you said, let alone how you said it? That's what it is like. When I finish writing, I have pages of comments and statements from the spirits. Not just on one subject but many subjects. I have mentioned to a few friends that it's like spirit has attention deficit disorder because they jump around so much.

Having a gold mine of information on subjects and people, I have taken to writing the person's name or subject in the margin for quick reference.

So, what, pray tell, am I being told? Um, well, I will tell you that I feel like spirit *tattles* on people. Some things are good, and some are, shall we say, not so good. If I get a message for one of my friends, I will send them a text that says, "MESSAGE DELIVERY!" and repeat the information I was given. I want to disclaim that I am not excluded from this either. I have been called out personally many a time! I get no free passes in this!

I hear happy things about people and hear the future paths of others. Those, by far, are the most fun messages to pass on. Then, there are the "other" ones. (Insert dramatic music for effect here.)

I have been told a lot of secrets. They are not my secrets. For example, I have heard that someone close to me has a child they know nothing about but are going to know soon. I have heard about the true heart desires of others in love and about their marriage. I say nothing. I just write all this down. If someone mentions something to me, I have proof. Anything that is validated later, I highlight.

I had about a two-week stint where I was told about a few pending deaths, and how they were going to happen. That information had me asking a lot of questions. Ethical questions. I do not think I am God. I do not control fate. Nor am I the only one who does this in the world! So that has me wondering if I should say something. What if I don't? I mean, technically, I have zero proof until it happens, right? I don't get dates or times. I just know who they have told me about and how it will happen. So, as I was showered with this information, I had to ponder the thought of if I say anything and what. Seriously, how does one handle this?

I was driving to the Rhine for the monthly Psychic Exchange Group meeting and was seriously trying to wrap my head around knowing this kind of information. What is my responsibility? Would I want to know? (Maybe?) I mean, seriously, we are all going to die. No one can cheat death. I'm just concerned about those left behind. I started talking out loud as I was driving, literally asking as if my spirit guides were all buckled into seat belts. "Do I have a responsibility to say something now that you told me?"

Let me tell you, no sooner than those words came out of my mouth, a car pulled up next to me on the highway with a perfectly placed bumper sticker on the left-side rear window that said "RESIST."

Instantly, a full belly laugh erupted from me! Good Lord, I had tears running down my face. It was a full-blown *cannot-stop-laughing-to-save-my-life* belly laugh. To quote Jeff Foxworthy, "Here's your sign!"

You see, if you look around, most of the time you get the answer. Seriously, spirit speaks to you all the time! Bumper stickers, license plates, words in songs that suddenly come on are all signs. You just have to pay attention!

I did have one more question for my spirit team before I went to bed that night. Why tell me if I wasn't supposed to do anything about it? (I think it was a fair question!) The answer they gave me was that they wanted to see how I felt about getting the information and what I would do about it. I would like to think that I passed the test.

After all, they are still telling me more secrets!

CHAPTER 14

"LIFE-GASMS"

LIFE-GASM | adjective | Word used to describe those moments when all is right in your world. The stars are aligned, the earth sits right on its axis, and your heart is just full of gratitude. A moment when you are fully present.

~ ~ ~

Ever had one of those life-gasm moments? I have! They don't happen too often, but when they do, they feel so powerful! Mostly, we experience them at times when something profound happens and you're so happy your heart could burst!

I decided I wanted to go to a good old-fashioned pumpkin patch instead of the grocery store to get a pumpkin for Halloween. I did this as a kid. Having relocated to North Carolina, I had the opportunity to go to an official pumpkin patch again!

Want pumpkin: will travel!

GPS set? CHECK! Gas in the tank? CHECK! Sunroof and windows open? CHECK! Tunes cranked up? CHECK! I plugged in the address of a local pumpkin patch, and I was off!

The weather was just beautiful! My windows were down. It was a cool temperature for the day and the trees were all in competition for the "most gorgeous" crown. It was fantastic! Eat your heart out, Florida friends!

It was still early and there was barely any traffic. I soaked up the sun on my face, the open highway, and listened to some fantastic tunes. The moment could have been a commercial!

I think it was one of many moments that just hit me. I was simply present. Appreciative. Grateful … Oh … SO … GRATEFUL!

Seriously, if you had met me one year before, you would not have recognized me! I started to reflect, then, on how far I had come in just one year.

I don't know about you, but once upon a time, I remember sitting in math class trying to take a test and I kept looking at the clock. (Algebra was not my favorite subject!) It moved so damn slow. Minutes felt like years! The insult to my frustration was that every time I looked at said clock, I saw the sign that the teacher placed above it: "Time will pass, will you?" Now chunks of time disappear. Poof! Gone. Evaporated. I mean, solid months and years seem to have gone by in a flash! Having said all that, one year prior, time was moving slowly. My soul felt singed by every single breathing moment of time during my divorce. Now, suddenly, there I was, just one year later, happy as a lark!

Yep, here I was singing at the top of my lungs with the windows down. Then, suddenly, I turned off the radio. I needed to say out loud a massive thank you to my angels who helped me get to that point. If it weren't for the help of my great-aunt and grandparents on the other side, I don't know if I could have made it. It was simply a LIFE-GASM moment. I wanted to give credit where credit was due. Was this the first time I said thank you? Oh, hell no! I say it all-the-time! I just tell them to suck it up and deal with the fact that I need to say it a lot! So far, they haven't told me to stop or that they are bored hearing it. So, I keep doing it!

Anyway, I said a few things out loud with a smile in my heart and then, to the left, a car passed by me, their license plate: MNT2BE!

I burst out laughing! It was a comment from the other side! My angels are really good at talking to me through signs.

It was truly awesome! It's only through reflection in the rearview mirror that you see how far you have traveled. I don't know where life is leading me, but I do know I'm on the right road and where I am at now is where I am meant to be.

CHAPTER 15

HOGWARTS BOUND!

Postcard

Well, technically, I am taking the bus there tomorrow, but I am currently in England! Trust me, I have run into the proverbial brick wall many times, but I've never managed to reach anything truly wonderful in haste. So, I will take the bus this time to play it safe!

Hogwarts is the unofficial nickname of the Arthur Findlay College in Stansted, England. Here, let me save you some googling time: *Arthur Findlay College is a college of spiritualism and psychic sciences at Stansted Hall in Stansted Mountfitchet, Essex, England. Stansted Hall was built in 1871, and the college was founded there in 1964. Wikipedia.*

Here's my backstory about how I got here. In readings that others did for me over the past few years, they told me repeatedly that they saw *large bookshelves and big desks*. They kept saying it looked like the Hogwarts campus in the very popular *Harry Potter* movies.

Being a lover of libraries, it made sense. It wasn't just one person who said this to me, so the seed was planted for that—or so I thought.

The words Arthur Findlay College kept popping up over and over again. I finally asked my angels if they wanted me to go, to please present the words to me again. Lo and behold, a day or two later I was running errands around town and started a new spiritually-based audiobook. In one of the first chapters, the author mentions that she went to the Arthur Findlay College. That, folks, is all it took. I booked two weeks back-to-back, flew across the pond to England for the first time in my life and here I am. I am officially in England going to Hogwarts tomorrow along with a few hundred other students from all over the world to learn and grow.

I am excited and a bit scared to be honest. These classes I am dipping my toes into are new territory for me. I know I am supposed to be here though. I feel it.

I quickly learned two things! The first one is that I am so going to be talking with a British accent by the end of this trip! (*Would you like a spot of tea?*) The second thing is that two weeks' worth of clothes weighs the same as scuba diving equipment and clothes for one week! Now you know!

CHAPTER 16

HOGWARTS LIFE

POSTCARD GREETINGS FROM ARTHUR FINDLAY COLLEGE!

(Aka Hogwarts!)

Let me tell you, I am having a blast. Trust me, it's work but it's work I like. We have 106 people in the class right now. I am in team Gryffindor.

Everyone is from everywhere. I'm not kidding! All over the world! I am so enjoying the accents of some of my new friends. In fact, I am having a hard time deciding which one I want to duplicate as my very own! My roommate speaks Italian with a French influence. I find ways to keep her talking so I can listen to her passionate verbalization. Then, there is Michelle from Dublin. OMG! I had her just talk trash and swear as I recorded her. She is a blast. Then, of course the *Downtown Abbey* dialect of England itself!

We are doing twelve-hour days here and they go by in a blink. Let me just say, I am so happy that I finally got the hint of resetting my internal clock before arriving! (I made myself go to bed at 7 p.m. and wake up at 2 a.m. to adjust to the five-hour time difference.) I would be a zombie had I not heeded spirit's warning. (Hallelujah and amen!)

There are so many cool things I'm experiencing. One is the greatest feeling of acceptance for me. There are unwavering amounts of support here. I have barely been able to blink, so I will just highlight some of the really cool aspects we have had the opportunity to experience.

We did spirit art. Sounds simple right? Hey, give me some finger paints and a wall and I will paint you a lovely picture! Not! We all showed up to a grand room in this mansion and settled into a seat at the table. We were all given blindfolds and immediately the jokes started about it being a *Fifty Shades of Grey* type of event. We were then teamed up and given pastels and paper. One of us went first and we listened to whatever spirit gave us to draw and did it. You let them guide your hands. My partner for this event was like freakin' Picasso! Seriously, my jaw just dropped. I told my spirit team that they needed to step it up as I was pretty sure my skills were still at a third-grade level. (My guide, Jean-Paul is a painter, so I had high hopes!) Blindfold in place, I saw the pictures in my mind that spirit wanted me to attempt, and my fingers went to work. Now, my drawing was no Salvador Dali, mind you, but I was pretty pleased! I drew a rose and some other pretty cool things! After we were both done, we were to give each other a reading based on the picture. I got rave reviews!

My partner read my picture and it shocked me how accurate she was. My picture is securely in my bag to be displayed on my refrigerator.

I am giving spirit a gold star!

Next up was spirit photography. Admit it, we have all done it. You aimed your camera into a cemetery to hopefully capture and see a cloudy mist of anyone or, at least, see if an orb showed up in a picture. Imagine eighteen of us in a group with flashes going off, trying to catch spirits in the sanctuary. At one point, it seemed like strobe lights. We were all seeing spots. The only thing I spotted in my pictures was my shiny forehead and something that resembled the Grinch. They said sometimes it takes a while to come through, so I will keep looking.

Another event was trance healing. Now, I don't know about you but the idea of being able to help others to heal, as well as myself, sounds pretty darn cool. We sat for a few moments when a random person in the class came and sat in front of you. Without seeing them, you give a message meant to help heal. You are guided to speak.

Thus far, one event that I fumbled with was—and you might laugh—tell the other person how wonderful you are. I'm going to preface this by saying I do not lack self-confidence. So, hear me out. This was a different spin. I don't know about you, but I do not go around saying, "*HI! Got five minutes? I need you to know how great I am!*" HEEELLLLLLL no! Not me! So, I go first. I'm thinking, I got this!

WRONG!

Two minutes in and I was running out of things to say. I floundered. The best I could come up with around the three-minute mark was that I made great sandwiches!

I was in complete awe of how I knew I was a good person yet could not come up with five minutes' worth of information to tell someone who didn't know me.

Then Ava, my partner, had her turn. She is in her mid-twenties and was so amazing, not only with what she said, but that she was so attuned to what she knew was wonderful about herself. I told the teacher that I wanted to be like Ava when I grew up! I think what hit me the most was that I should have said everything she said—and I didn't. I was everything she said—yet couldn't remember it. Yup! I have work to do. If you think it is so easy, try it.

One more thing I will address before I sign off for the night: you would think if you were in a class of 106 mediums that you could get the inside scoop on things, right? Nope! (Insert five-year-old stomping feet, arms crossed, and pouting face.) To me, it's like sitting in the middle of an electrical field but nobody is letting me have electricity.

As frustrating as this is for me at times, there are times that spirit will hide things from you just so you go through the experience. It's about the journey to the answer, not the answer itself. They just want you to know that they are there and to simply trust. Well, trust me, I have tried a few times already. No one is spilling the beans yet! I will keep trying and keep you posted!

CHAPTER 17

HOGWARTS WEEK 1 – CHECK!

Postcard

Week 1: Done! Holy cow. What a week! The Experimental Trance Mediumship course was challenging at times but seriously cool to learn. I met some of the most amazing people and had outstanding conversations. The guidance, readings, and tutors that I had were so healing and helpful. I experienced a side of myself that I hadn't seen in a very-long-time. I understand things I couldn't wrap my head around before. I am on the right path and excited about where it will lead me.

The last few days of week one here at Hogwarts had a few more tricks to teach and things for me to experience. It sure kept me on my toes!

Cabinet work: This I had never done before and, honestly, like hadn't even heard of. To paint a picture for you, it's a portable closet with three sides and the fourth/front open. There is a red-light shining in. The person in the closet sits on a chair and goes into a trance state. The closet allows you to feel the energy around you. And-you-do. It's also amazing how your eyes can play tricks. As people blended their energy with spirits, some of their faces appeared to change shape. We sat in observation and used our abilities to vocalize what we saw and felt. You could feel the cold swoop in. You could feel, hear, and see. It was really, really different to do and experience. Most of all, it was incredible to feel the energy you actually have because it was in a confined space.

Electronic voice phenomenon: The entire class divided up and groups of us went to different places in the mansion. There was a control list of questions that each group asked. Then, collectively as a group, we added a few more questions of our own. We all used our phones as the tutor asked the questions one by one. Then, we listened to see if any voices came through. No one had anything to report from OUR group, but we were encouraged to listen again with earphones after we retired for the evening. Collectively as a class, a few other groups heard distinctive words spoken in response to the questions. Once I got back to my room, I used my own headphones to listen and on one of my recordings I heard: "Give me back my life." Oddly enough, I wasn't freaked out. I handed my phone to my roommate, and she also heard the same. I marked the time down and told my teacher. I am going to hook it up to louder speakers when I get home. My neighbors won't like it but at least I will reconfirm what I heard!

Table walking: I didn't participate in this elective class because there were other classes that I felt were more important for me to take. During teatime and meal breaks we all compared stories and some of them would make your jaw drop. The table walking one was insane! So-much-energy! I took a video of another student's video of the table walking. To explain what this is, the energy of the students blended with spirit causes the table to wobble and "walk." It really was quite a sight to see how *much* it was dancing all around! The video showed it wobbling out the classroom door! It reminded me of the cartoon *Beauty and the Beast*!

Automatic writing: I have done this quite a few times before and I feel very comfortable with it. The exercise for class was to pick a random number. Someone else in the room had the same number but you didn't know who. You were to focus on the unknown recipient and allow spirit to help you write out a message to the other person from them. No problem! Have pen: will write! After, you find the person with the matching number and give them your message. I am still in awe of what I wrote and how utterly appropriate it was for the recipient. My matching number was a lovely lady from Germany. She said my message was spot on and I couldn't be happier. She then gave me the message she received from my grandmother for me, who passed away about a year and a half ago. Grandma sang my praises for what I have been doing this week along with other evidential information. I so love my grandma!

Trance class: If I had to say that there was only one moment that made this week over the top, I would be fibbing. This next one was pretty high up there though. In class, I did a reading for Caroline. We were each supposed to talk about a loved one who had crossed over and build the energy up. After, we went into a trance state and relayed any additional messages that they wanted to send. Caroline's nan (grandmother) was so warm and had such love! I know I said a few things, but it was also the pictures she was showing me. The evidence that it was her. I was so damn happy! WOO-HOO! I finally got evidence! Like, you have no idea how happy I was to get confirming messages that were validated. (My signs workbook I filled out in the park before coming here paid off!) I was so happy about this! Caroline then did the same for me and my grandmother came through again giving evidence. I know she is still around me all the time! The message I received was so heartfelt and awesome.

This morning was hard because the week of courses was over. We all packed our suitcases, shared hugs, and exchanged emails. I had to part ways with some of the most AH-MAZING friends as most of them left to go back to their respective parts of the world. There were so many classmates I never got a chance to talk to from other classes. One thing we all had in common though was we all shared the same love of helping and healing through spirit.

Although I packed up like the rest of my classmates, I am only changing rooms and roommates. A handful of us are staying on for another week and another set of classes.

I am still here. I can't wait to start my second week at Hogwarts!

CHAPTER 18

HOGWARTS COURSE 2

Part 1

Postcard

I really thought I had a grip on my emotions but everyone I knew left today. I am here still but starting all over again with course number two.

I have a new course syllabus for the week, tutors, roommate, and lodging location. My inner five-year-old wants to go hide in the corner and wait for my mom because I feel like I have been abandoned. What is wrong? Seriously, I have no clue. I just feel very quiet and alone.

I attribute it to a few things like being overly tired, meeting fresh faces to seek alliances with again, and questioning myself if I have the talent necessary to appease the new tutors for the week. I think I need a nap. Rest assured; I pulled my big girl panties up. I got this.

This week's accommodations are in the mansion. Can I just stop right here and give a huge shout-out to Elisha Otis, the creator of the elevator? I'm not sure if I just lost muscle mass suddenly in a week or if my suitcase suddenly gained twenty pounds. There was an internal agreement that, should my options amount to dragging my suitcase up two flights of stairs, I was going to throw most of my clothes out and opt for whatever I could carry.

In making that agreement with myself, I didn't realize that I would have been in competition with a couple staying here who have been wearing the exact same clothes for the last five days. We question if their luggage is lost. It's become Groundhog Day seeing them every day.

This week's course is Advance Mediumship Training. It's very different than last week. Here are a few highlights so far:

I discovered that the mansion where the college is located had been used as a military hospital in the past. I also found out that when they built the staircase, the center of it was kept big enough for and in the shape of a coffin. Should a soldier pass away, they lowered him down the middle of the staircase. Respectfully, I bet they wished they had an elevator!

My room is on the second floor of the mansion this week, with the potty down the hall from it. Your door locks behind you, so don't forget your key! You are dealing with multiple spirits in the college. I now have about thirty steps to get to said potty in the middle of the night. (Hey, I went to summer camp—I got this, right?) Except now you have to actually go potty in the middle of the night.

Key? CHECK. Open door quietly so you don't wake your roommate? CHECK. Walk down the hall to the potty and realize you could see a spirit at any moment—with a full bladder? Holy crap! Let me just say, I chanted down the hall, "*Please don't let me see a spirit—please don't let me see a spirit"*—more than I care to admit. So far, so good!

Ghosts of the past: UGH, this one was/is—well, this was a difficult assignment for me. In this class, one of your classmates sits in front of you and connects with a spirit that knows you. So, my classmate, Monica, sits down and brings forth my stepfather who died a few years ago. Through Monica, he wanted to tell me that he was sorry for the abuse I suffered while my mother was working. That reading was *not* fun for me. Thank goodness the classroom had many boxes of tissues!

Team of family cheerleaders: I have to laugh about what has happened the last few days. First of all, I am very grateful that I have not known much loss in my life thus far. The important passed-on family members are my grandparents and great-aunt. They have been so damn awesome in helping me this week.

So, in this class, my grandmother made her first appearance. The tutor was chatting and one of the other students in class interrupted her and said that my grandmother insists on speaking up and has been "waiting patiently" for the teacher to be done. (I can picture my grandmother saying this!) The tutor urged him to go ahead. Mike looked at me and said, "*Your grandmother wants you to know that she has your back!*" How cool is that?

Another student then said that he got a message of a lot of energy coming in and that 80 percent was directed toward MOI. I really appreciated it, considering that forty-five minutes earlier, I was standing outside verbally reminding my angels and spirit guides that they needed to step up help for me this week! Message sent; message received.

My great-aunt Arline came through with all sorts of evidential things for me and she even called me gorgeous. My grandfather was my partner helping me with a few other different exercises today as well. I love my spirit team and am so grateful for their continued help!

Mealtimes this week are like a high school lunchroom. We are all comparing stories and trading information and opinions. We learned that one of the ladies at our table does forensic profiling mediumship. What an intriguing round of discussions that brought up! It seemed fascinating!

One of the other girls then mentioned that she had done trance forensic mediumship a few times. Without skipping a beat, she mentioned that after she could taste the gasoline being poured down a women's throat during one trance state, and another where the subject had bricks tied around her throat and was dumped down a well, she said never again. Imagine the horror on our faces hearing these stories! (Note to self: cross those careers off the list!)

We have three days left until this class is over. There have been belly dancing lessons in the bar and an elaborate debate about a classmate who has a Ouija board printed on her shirt and did that mean she wants everyone to put their hand on her shirt to "get or give a message"? We have also channeled our childish antics by watching a patron, commenting on how fabulous his hair was. We have gelled together very well this week and no doubt there will be more antics to report!

CHAPTER 19

HOGWARTS COURSE 2

Part 2

Postcard

What a week! I actually had to refer back to a written list I created for the second half so I wouldn't forget anything. Thus, these are random experiences and observations.

Meditation: You know, I'm getting pretty good at that part! Every morning, everyone would meet to do morning meditation after breakfast for thirty minutes. (I have come such a long way from the five minutes when I started!) The first few minutes, when we all were quiet, you heard a symphony of gurgles and squeals of everyone's breakfast digestion. There were a few times that, collectively, our group would seriously fight a fit of uncontrollable giggles. Ever had that moment? The moment you are supposed to be super quiet and serious, and you can't contain your laughter? That was us. Ultimately, though, I swear they would start the meditation, thirty minutes would evaporate, and we were mentally back in the room.

Groundhog Day with the repeating clothes: Just because you were dying to get an update about the couple wearing the same clothes, I will fill you in. Yes, for eight days straight, they wore the exact same clothes EVERY-SINGLE-DAY. No one ever knew if their luggage was lost or not. What we did find out is that the husband was suffering from some type of mental illness and could not be left alone at all, so his wife brought him to the course to wander around during our class times. He has some memory issues. Possibly, wearing the same clothes was meant to help the husband remember who she was.

What you present to the world versus your soft underbelly: Boy, this was so real for me this week in more ways than one. We all have this "persona" we present to the world. It is a version of ourselves depending on what is needed at the moment we interact with others. Ever see the meme "You never know what someone else is going through, so be kind"? This week was a perfect example of that for me.

As we got up to give messages to our fellow classmates from their loved ones, inadvertently, many of us were brought to tears as our wounds and trials were exposed by some of the most endearing messages gifted to us by our loved ones in spirit.

There is a lot of love and appreciation from the spirit world all the time. Each message unfolded a layer of our true self that no one knew about. In a way, the spirits were reaching out to say we know you are hurting, and we support you.

What we learned is that if you are still upset about something or were triggered by the message, it was a notice to work on letting go and releasing the pain associated with the occurrence. That's much easier said than done! We are all a work in progress. It explains why there were multiple boxes of tissues around the rooms! I certainly used my quota. Guess what the college is getting for Christmas? More tissues!

Student demonstrations: Each night, a few students volunteered to stand up in front of fellow peers and deliver messages from loved ones who have crossed over to the students in the audience.

I did platform work in my group but not in front of the entire class. I was the MC for a few of these. I channeled my inner Vanna White, introducing my classmates. It was interesting to watch the variety of ways messages were presented. I know I want to have energy and humor in my delivery.

Some were like the Energizer Bunny: fast-talking, quickly pacing back and forth, like a passionate lawyer presenting their case. On the opposite side of the spectrum were some so still and quiet from stage shock.

I watched the audience's reactions to the different ways evidence was presented and took note of what I best resonated with. I also learned that there were pre-planted "body snatchers," people who, no matter who could identify with the evidential information, would claim it also fit them. Some sat in front with arms folded across their chest, presenting a very closed-off person.

This practice was for us to learn to dig deeper and find something unique to present—like a memory for evidence. For example, not using general information such as: I have a woman present, and she has grey hair and is hunched over with a cane.

Instead, use unique information like: I have a woman here and she is sharing with me the memory of you playing bingo together at the wooden kitchen table, using pennies as markers, and a dog knocking the table over, scattering everything.

Laughter: Some of the extra fun demonstrations were those involving language barriers. They acted out a word they did not know! I gave them so much credit for their effort! My roommate acted out a chipmunk, because of the language barrier. She did not know how to translate bucked teeth and had us all in stitches! It could easily have been a game of charades at times. Rest assured, it lightens the mood quite a bit to laugh with the medium. There were more over-the-top moments where the demonstrating medium truly felt and grasped a strong personality of the spirit. Holy hell—we had so much fun with that! In my class, Meena got up and presented a spirit that had *really* big breasts. Like, so big that her back hurt and she compensated by walking funny and was also a chain smoker. We were doubled over with nonstop laughter.

I was called out by a dear, deceased friend and ex sister-in-law, Dorothy, who said through the medium that *she sees me eating a lot of chocolate lately at my house.* When everyone looked at me to validate the information, I must have looked like a deer in headlights—talk about being outed in front of the class! I just looked at the medium and said, "*I may or may not resonate with that statement!*" We laughed so hard that day! It was awesome to use the tissues to dry up tears from laughter. Message received and delivered! (PS I'm out of chocolate!)

Kindergarten Evidential Mediumship class graduation: Even though this course was for intermediate-level mediumship, the course administrator put our collective class into subgroups of like experience to enhance our abilities based on skill level. Fair enough! We were all there to learn. There were some in our group who were actively practicing mediums and were there to enhance their abilities. We called them the "seniors." Some of the mediums acted like they were going on TV in the next few weeks! There was a group that was more middle-of-the-road but still actively working. They had mad skills. Personally, like a lot of us, I saw no difference in the more advanced classmates or honestly being better at all!

Then there was my group I endearingly called the kindergarten class. In my group, we certainly could do just as much as the other groups, but we had questions about techniques that would have probably bored some of the more seasoned mediums. Our teacher, Sally, was amazing. She told us that she truly felt that we were just as good as the seniors, if not better and she was so proud of our accomplishments. We appreciated that comment from her as it was a boost to our confidence! We took a group photo together, exchanged email addresses and phone numbers to keep in touch.

Cemetery & Church: One day during a break, everyone at my lunch table and I went over to the onsite cemetery and church. Built in 1691, the church was truly intriguing and amazing. Some of the tombstones were from 1600–1700 as well. The final night before the course was complete, I felt unwell, but my lunch table went back over to the cemetery to take photos at night, as it is considered a very active spot. You should see the photos! Thick white streaks emanated from a lot of the graves. It was show-and-tell at breakfast. Seriously cool!

Miscellaneous: One of the course administrators, Paul Jacobs, was leaving the college to promote himself on tour. They threw a party in his honor one evening, which was fun. Of course, some of the decorations were helium balloons. So, before meditation the next morning, most of the balloons were still floating. I had an audience and took advantage of speaking the beginning words for the group meditation we were about to do but, in a helium,-induced tone. Further encouraged by an uproar of laughter, I also did my very special camp song, *"God Bless My Underwear"*—in helium-speak. I don't drink in excess, don't smoke—but I love a helium-filled balloon!

Final: In summary, it was an amazing two weeks. I learned a lot. I grew a tremendous amount. The friendships and connections that I made all around the world will stay with me forever. It was like having a slumber party every night. Twelve-hour days felt like nothing. I adored my roommates and new friends. My tutors were outstanding for having helped us collectively as a group but also individually. Having also been exposed to other tutors' teaching ways, I know who resonates best for my particular way of learning for future classes. I understand why so many have gone back year after year. I no longer feel like a new student but a college alumnus. I said it before and I will say it again, HOGWARTS RULES!

CHAPTER 20

COMMUNITY BENEFITS – FINDING MY PEOPLE

After my two-week trip to Arthur Findlay College in England, I came back to the USA ready to go. Not only did I want to practice what I learned but also learn more!

One of the things they encouraged us to do while there was to "sit in the power" for thirty minutes each morning. What's that you ask? Well, it's quieting your mind and heart, but with a group. It is blending your energy with the group's energy. I am so glad I practiced meditating on my own before I got there so I could do this.

Anyway, I questioned during the two weeks if I really could quell my inner thoughts for longer than fifteen minutes. Could I do this alone at home? Yes, but teachers encouraged us to do it with others if possible. They explained that collectively, energetically charged friends would amplify the experience. Well, alrighty then! I was on it!

As far as groups around me at home go, I didn't think there was much around, so I looked to the local Meet Up groups again. There were a handful of people who promoted sitting in the power.

Translation: Pay them $25 to sit in silence with others, in their living room.

Oh, hell no! Something just felt wrong about that to me. Seriously! They wanted me to take time out of my day to drive to their house, sit in their living room in silence, and then pay *them* $25? Nope! Nope and hell nope!

I also realized that the classes I were taking locally were too short. By the time everyone got there, some often late, it felt like the class was over and we were all just getting started.

I contacted one of the teachers I worked with locally and explained my plight. I said to her, "I'm going to start a practice group! It will not be a teaching group but a safe place where we can practice what you teach us and what we have already learned. Was it OK with her to solicit the people in the class she was teaching?"

She was encouraging and said yes. At one of her next classes, I mentioned that I was going to spearhead a "practice group" and did anyone want to practice?

WHOA! Everyone in the class signed up! Thus, was born what we fondly called the Woo-Woo Practice Group.

I was the head honcho, coordinating the times, places and sending out notifications. We would all gather together, do a group meditation (aka sitting in the power), and the feeling we all got after doing this together? WHOA! It was a very intense power for sure! We all would comment on how it felt like we were vibrating with energy! It was so profound for all of us!

Word spread and more people joined our group. One talented lady in our group called us all "Super-Friends." Another got a drop-in message that "this group was divinely orchestrated, and it was meant to be for us all to be together."

No money exchanged hands at all. It was free to participate. We kept our group open to those who were at or around the same skill level as well. We were not a teaching group, so those who joined needed to have taken classes or had natural talent. There were many who wanted to "try and see if they could" but I just encouraged them to take classes and come back when they were further along.

I am a huge advocate of an "equal exchange of energy." In our group we felt safe to exchange opinions and offer ideas regarding the delivery and accuracy of the messages received for each other.

Everyone has different talents in our group. We all encourage each other to try different modalities if something piques our interest. If someone read cards but takes an interest in pendulum work, that's what they practiced for the day on someone. If you practiced mediumship but wanted to try channeling—that's what you practiced. If you were skilled in automatic writing but wanted to utilize palmistry, then you could. It was a safe place to practice anything you wanted and there was no time frame for what you had to do. If you could stay for two to three hours, great! Everyone got a chance to practice what they were learning and also feel safe from ridicule.

At one point, the group of us were consistent in meeting regularly and happy with the accuracy of the messages we were getting for each other. It was like we all were leveling up!

As a group, we decided to bring strangers in for an impromptu psychic fair. It was an offer only extended to our friends and family for free. We needed new participants we knew nothing about to receive messages for. At the end of each of our readings for them, we gave them an anonymous survey to fill out, as an equal exchange of our energy. We discussed as a group what we wanted to know from these surveys. Making it anonymous also helped the ones receiving the reading (aka "sitter") be more honest with us from an outsider's point of view.

No money exchanged hands. It was a practice run for all of us. We all learned a lot about our own energy, clearing ourselves from the prior reading, and what sitters wanted to know from us as readers. There were a few hiccups in doing this, but we all learned a lot from what we did. I still have my surveys to this day!

In doing this, it also gave us the courage to start to venture out on our own. Some started businesses to give readings in the modality of their choice. A few have written books. Most have incorporated their talents as an extension of what they do for work.

We all are still "practicing." There is no diploma that you have reached the top. Sometimes, you can get so good at one modality but suddenly something else strikes your fancy and you want to practice.

One of the benefits of us all being together is the support we give each other. That in itself is so amazing! It is like having an opportunity to get guidance from each other's spirit guides. After all, they are all friends now as well! If any of us are not sure what direction to take? We ask if anyone can "tap in" and receive the answer.

There are a few who have had a friend or family member go missing for a spell and we would all "tap in" to find them (remote viewing). Should one of us need some extra strength or healing—we put it out there to the group and the texts and personal calls come flooding in. It's like the presidential red phone of support.

One of the coolest things, hands down, is the drop-in messages that we receive for each other. Mind you, in our everyday lives we do not interact with each other daily. Put us in a room together and you visually couldn't tie us together. Our spirit guides though? They must hang out together on the other side. They have got all of our backs!

It was strange for some of us to receive these at first. Ever just start thinking about someone and suddenly they call or reach out to you? That's what it is like. Except this is taking it one step further. We receive messages to give to each other. Their face would pop up in our mind and then a message would follow.

All of us are human. We experience trials, tribulations, and heartaches that we don't share or disclose to others. This group, though, was like a spy among spies. Man, you cannot have an issue without someone reaching out, saying, "OK, what's going on? I received a message for you!" Have I mentioned that spirit can be a tattletale?

No lie, that's how a lot of them start. Are they accurate in doing so? Oh yeah! Oh my gosh—and random too!

One night, spirit woke me up repeatedly between two and three in the morning. Yes, you read that correctly—AM—to give me drop-in messages for someone. I fired off emails with snippets to that person for an hour.

Another time, I took a walk in one of the local parks and got a drop-in message for another fellow woo-woo group participant. Accuracy? One hundred percent spot on, even though it made zero sense to me. Mind you, these drop-in messages have taken some getting used to because they are so random and often make no sense to me when I get them. Ultimately, the intuitive nudges are at the right time for the person receiving the message. When I am knee-deep in thought or frustrated, I can't receive unbiased messages for myself, so this helps a great deal when my friends reach out to me, too!

Alas, it has been discussed within our group that we all question if we need to reach out sometimes but how spirit will *not* let it go until we do. It's like an annoying mosquito that you hear, can't see, and wonder where it's going to land next. Timing though? Perfecto! One was so perfectly timed she told me that I saved her life, *literally*. I will let you figure that one out.

I want to stress that not all messages or the timing of them are when conditions are dire. Some are simply guidance that you need to get off a hamster wheel or break through a proverbial glass ceiling so you can take the next step.

I swear, in my head I see the visual of all the angels yelling down at us for the direction we need to take. When we don't get the message, they use their "phone a friend" option and make those friends deliver the message to you. I cannot tell you how many times I have delivered messages to others, and others delivered messages to me, that evoke thigh-slapping laughter. Seriously, you can't make this stuff up! It certainly gets us out of our heads and onto the next part.

The gratitude I hear from the person receiving the drop-in message is often so heartfelt, though. I have learned to truly embrace my inner voice of knowing and if I need to do something further with it. I no longer question when I get a random message no matter what it is. I just pay attention and ask if further action is needed on my part. If there is, I do it. I have learned that the accuracy of the need far outweighs the possible embarrassment if for some reason I am wrong.

The community I started out of necessity has been paramount in my growth. Feeling safe to share the learning journey with other like-minded individuals is so helpful to me. Sitting in the power is necessary work so that you know what is you, and what is spirit. The practice group of woo-woo super-friends still work together to this day.

So, dear reader, I encourage you to find like-minded people to work with as well or start your own group. We are *all* microphones for spirit whether you realize it or not or whether you have any formal training. Paying attention to these nudges when they happen is paramount. Being open to receiving a message from someone else can be extremely beneficial as well. You always have free will to make decisions though. More doors will open for you as you travel on this journey. There is much to learn and, honestly? The "teachers" are pretty darn cool!

CHAPTER 21

REMOTE VIEWING – DID YOU SEE IT?

There was a speaker at a local spiritualist gathering on remote viewing. She was fascinating to me! I sat in the front row, notebook and pen in hand, taking notes!

Her presentation was very intriguing! She spoke of the FBI contacting her and only giving her a random file number. She then contacted a select group of other remote viewers from around the world to help, also only giving them the file number. Each person would focus their energy and relay their findings to her. After she compiled the group's findings, she would send her report back to the FBI.

She was never told or given any validation on what the group produced or if they were even close or not. On occasion, the government or special forces group would inadvertently let her know if, and how, her findings helped them in their quest. I would assume that because of the number of times they contacted her, her group's findings must have been accurate!

She spoke of how this work was helpful in many different ways.

She spoke of missing children's cases she participated in. She could see them being abducted and see through the child's eyes what was happening and report to local authorities or parents. I decided at that point that if ever asked, I would need to be in a good place mentally to receive this kind of information. Note taken!

She also has been contracted by large corporations to look for flaws in their systems, and/or evidence of things and events. She mentioned that although she was contracted by these corporations, she drew the line at revealing information about the personal lives of the employees if it was not pertinent to the inquiry. She felt the employee's privacy needed to be respected no matter what.

A lot of this made me think about how many ways this gift could be used but also abused! Dang!

The first half of her talk was over, but she gave a file number before the break to those of us in the audience. She invited us to focus and see what information we could come up with. Challenge accepted!

I was excited! My first "case"! I calmed my breathing, focused on the case number, and wrote down and drew what came to my mind's eye. I actually had quite a few things come to mind. I drew some of the pictures out, wrote out words and then went on a break myself.

Upon the continuation of the talk, the speaker asked if anyone wanted to give it a go as to what the picture of the case number entailed. Well, let me tell you, my hand shot right up.

She chose me first. I told her I saw a mountain; it looked like a mountain in Bora Bora to me, but it was a mountain. I also saw sand or a path, an infinity symbol (figure eight that is sideways), glasses that someone would be wearing, and a few other things.

She then went around the room with the most stoic expression on her face. There was no hint of validation for anyone's answers! I was trying to read her body language, but she was a tough cookie and gave nothing away.

There were maybe fewer than ten of us who attempted this exercise in the audience. She then proceeded to show the actual pictures in a slide show pertaining to the case number she gave us. It was a mountain with snow on it along a road! One other person and I were the closest! I was plum proud of myself!

But at first, I discounted my findings. Spirit nudged me and said to pause and think about it a bit more. So, after further thought, I realized a few things. My picture or symbol of a mountain was that in Bora Bora at the moment. Just because there was snow versus sand did not make my picture of a mountain any less of a mountain! Spirit then reminded me of my signs book. Again, pointing out that I had the right word, but my sign to express the word was different than someone else. It was perfectly OK! OK, I felt better.

It fascinated me even further because of the next few cases she described. She presented another case she was involved with, described her remote viewing findings and then showed pictures of what she was talking about. In those pictures were indeed items I drew on my break. One was a missing man who had *glasses* on his head. There was another picture that had the infinity shape in it. I not only got visions of the case she asked us to work on over the break, but future items in slides this lady used.

Am I perfect at this gift, or can I snap my fingers and make it happen instantly on command? Not just yet! Therein lies my journey of further discovery! How these abilities can be used is very intriguing and I see how they can indeed be helpful!

I also learned that those who specialize in the remote viewing arena have a very distinct process and procedure they follow when they "tap in." It's not the random rudimentary doodles that I did. She offered a training class over the following weekend for those wanting to learn the specific process I assume all trained remote viewers follow. I considered attending to get further training, but there wasn't a strong draw to it for me. I was just happy I learned about this, and doodle or not, I get information!

CHAPTER 22

HELLO, I AM A DECK-O-HOLIC

Hello, my name is Buyer, and I am a deck-o-holic. It has been four days since my last purchase. (The crowd replies: HELLO, BUYER!)

Oh, I love-me a good oracle card deck. They come in all shapes and sizes, but I gravitate toward the ones that fit comfortably in the palm of my hand. After handling quite a few, I have noted the ones most appealing to me, the ones with a smooth glossy finish that slide easily when shuffled. (Note to self: dumping corn starch onto a nonglossy deck to make them side better does *not* work!)

I love decks with character. I adore colorful, artistic pictures that sometimes make you think a little deeper. For example, Ciro Marchetti has a deck called Oracle of Visions. This is quite literally one of my top two favorite decks. It features Victorian carnival and theatrical images. No message is written on the card, so you look at it for symbolism. Sometimes, the message is obvious and sometimes it is the little images in the pictures that tell the truer story.

Decks speak to everyone differently. Your intuition about the deck seeps into your consciousness. I typically don't buy a deck unless I see it in person. It must feel right. It needs to appeal to my creative side as well as my intellect. The meanings of the cards individually and collectively must stand out to me in some way, shape, or form. It's a feeling I get holding them. Energy. Buying a box of cards without being able to open or see the images on the cards just seems wrong for me, personally. I have picked up many decks based on popular names, and they just don't resonate.

Most often, each deck will also come with a complementary book that goes along with it offering individual explanations of each card. Trust me, there are days that I am not in a contemplative thinking mood and need to get right to the heart of the matter. So, I open the book to see what it says about the card. This also allows me to possibly discover a deeper meaning of the card, which I might not have given thought to otherwise.

I started many years ago with the Rider Waite Tarot Deck. It was my desperate attempt to understand more about a relationship I was involved with that I could not make sense of. Goodness, I still have a hard time with that deck but as time has gone on, I don't care how you spin it—The Tower card is not a good card! Seriously, I have had a few readers try to put a positive spin on that card to no avail. Then, others have literally slid it under other cards in front of me while giving me a reading, to avoid talking about it. Seriously? Like I didn't see them do it! HA!

Sometimes I know that the message is literally and figuratively right in front of me, but I can't see it. It's hard to do a spread for myself. At times, it seemed my rose-colored glasses were superglued to my face for some reason. (Look, the Tower card just has a small crack in it, and we can fix it! Not!) So, I have put that deck away and pulled it out more times than I care to admit hoping for a different outcome. It is still a goal of mine to truly understand the deck further, but bigger projects are on my plate right now.

I have since graduated to oracle card decks. Aah, I found my happy place and have settled in quite nicely! It's my private addiction. I-LOVE-ME-SOME-ORACLE-CARDS. I adore the messages that they offer. Some people say that when you get a deck, you should look at every single individual card and get a feeling for it. If I looked at the deck in person and it resonated with me, I personally didn't need to look at every individual card. I saw what I needed to see, and if it resonated with me, I was happy. Should I see at least a few cards in the deck that I liked, I would buy it. I prefer that some of the cards remain a surprise anyway because I read more intuitively.

Everyone has their own routines to get a card from the deck. I shuffle them and ask for a message from my higher self or something that the spirit world wants me to know. I will ask for three cards. HO-LY cow—how scary accurate they are some days. It is as if spirit knocks them out of my hand as it is their chance to be up front and just tell me what I need to know or work on. It avoids many hours of guessing or trying to look through rose-colored glasses instead of seeing the clearer picture.

There have been many times, honestly, that I don't like the answer I receive through the oracle cards. Spirit does not care if I don't like the answer. They still tell me. Some days I channel my inner, mouthy five-year-old know-it-all and point-blank tell my spirit guides this. To my surprise (not!) they will give me the same messages until I pay attention and/or correct it. Once I do, they leave that subject alone. Regardless, it is done out of love. Just remember that there are no accidents or coincidences. You are meant to see and receive any message you get.

I have had days where I look at the card, don't want to deal with the message, and put it away. Guess what? Sixty-eight cards in a deck, shuffled, split, shuffled again, and the next day I will get the same damn card. I thought I would outwit spirit and have switched decks completely! I shuffle that deck and will get a like card on the same subject. In fact, I have mentioned to a few of my friends that I have thought honestly about marking on the book page that comes with the deck exactly how many times the same cards surface. If nothing else, it plants a seed (or a thorn), until you address what you are avoiding.

In my world so far, the cards I pull are very rarely unpleasant! Ever seek a further explanation of a path you should follow? How about the answer to a burning question? Admit it, some days it would be nice if spirit would just tell you every single answer. No guessing. No wondering. Then, some days you just need a hug, a word of encouragement, or a pat on the back. Oracle decks offer me those.

Regardless, I seek the unique expressions and words offered by the decks I have chosen for my personal growth. To me, each one is exciting and new. They help me. Often, it is not what you say but how you say it that means the most. There is no cookie-cutter rule for these decks. I get exactly what I need, in the way I need to hear it.

So back to my addiction. In one year, I may or may not have acquired an embarrassing number of amazing decks. I seek the unique and profound illustrations and messages themed in each. I love every one of them in their own way. Every trip I go on, I take a few with me. I also seem to bring a few more home. My collection is growing. I don't have every deck memorized. They feel new all over again, every time I open the box they came in. They help me talk about a story. My story.

CHAPTER 23

YOU HAVE ONE JOB: BE HAPPY

It is pretty cool that this can apply to all of us in many situations! It is now getting closer to the end of the year, so I want to put a new spin on New Year's resolutions. Hear me out!

We all have been asked at one time or another what we want to have, do, acquire, and accomplish at the start of a new year. Most of us have a grandiose-o list and all the mustered-up gumption to achieve it. We'll talk about how this year is going to be the year of change, sharing our plans with others like trading cards.

Did you know that statistically 80 percent of us lose our resolve by February? I'm not being a Debbie-Downer here, it's a fact! The best-laid plans are forgotten, and we get back on that same old hamster wheel of life. UGH!

A few years ago, someone enlightened me that it is not my job to make everyone happy. Who knew? Obviously, not me! I was a people pleaser extraordinaire after all! They really pushed the issue that my only responsibility was to take care of myself, and the other adults in my life were responsible for themselves. I was reminded that I did not come into this world with a list pinned to my skin that said:

She is to work, sacrifice and live her life to make the following people happy: (fill in blank).

Trust me, it took more than a few moments to wrap my head around this bit of information, for some reason. Once I got it through my thick head, I started exercising that option in my life. This was seriously enlightening to me. Mind you, with all the free time I had by not trying to make everyone else happy, spirit put in front of me the statement and challenge:

YOU ONLY HAVE ONE JOB TODAY: MAKE YOURSELF HAPPY.

(Insert dramatic music for effect) So, I am only in charge of making MOI, happy. Hmmm, is it really that simple? Well, it is supposed to be. Do I make it that easy for myself? No!

For some reason, my angels put this in front of me to address. There are no coincidences or accidents, trust me. This statement, though, was like reading a foreign language at that moment.

I thought I was pretty happy but deep down, I knew I had more work to do in this department. So, being the contemplative question for the moment, I do what I do best and wrote on a large wipe board with colorful markers: What do I need to do today to be really happy? Then, I proceeded to walk past it five million times and ponder. What in the tarnation was being really happy to me now? (Insert *Jeopardy* music here.) I felt like I was a happy person in general, but

I think spirit wanted me to raise my level to more than just maintaining the status quo.

The definition of what being happy to me changes moment by moment, day by day, and year by year. What made me happy yesterday isn't as profound or exciting today. Want me to prove it?

Ever have a life-gasm moment and go back to experience it again—same everything—and the magic you felt isn't the same? There you go! Same thing. What changed? YOU.

So, I challenged every statement or offer: if it didn't make me happy and bring me joy, then my answer was no.

Was this going to make some people mad around me? Yep! But again, was it my job to make them happy? NO! The challenge was to find my personal happiness in every moment. Not when I finally get to some unknown milestone. Mentally this mode of operation felt pretty freeing to me. I was onto something.

I took my soul out of the box of "expectations," and sat it on a proverbial chair in front of me in search of an honest answer. I asked what it needed to be really happy again. You know what? My soul told me. I actually listened. Yes, for the first time in a very long time I really listened.

What came to mind, as examples, was that I was really happy when I went for a walk or spent time outside. I felt happy when I made a phone call to someone I wanted to talk to. I felt joy when I took the time to just be still with my phone off, color in a coloring book or do something artistic while listening to my favorite music. I adored having a cup of coffee, reading a book of my choosing, or taking extra time for self-care. My heart felt alive when I gave back by volunteering and gave to others of my own free will.

Although I learned of current-day examples, I was reminded for the future to be present and look for things that made me happy in the moment. Not postpone being happy until tomorrow or next week. As some would say, stop and smell the roses.

I tasked myself to try this for one week. This was seriously an accomplishment for me. I felt lighter in my heart. I did it again for a second week. Everything I did or said, I applied the question, WILL-THIS-MAKE-ME-HAPPY?

I was on a roll. I realized I wasn't waking up stressed. I felt more at peace. I had gotten off the hamster wheel of life. My happiness level was leveling up every day.

I am not going to write about a specific road map to happiness as there is no one-size-fits-all answer. Another pearl of wisdom I learned in doing this is that if you still are unsure about what happy is for you, try instead looking at what makes you UN-happy. Then the opposite will tell you what will. Write out or speak the positive version.

Do you know what being genuinely happy looks like from the outside in? If you don't know what that answer could be, get your photo albums/pictures out. That's your proof. You can see it in yourself, what you look like when you are truly happy or just faking a smile for the camera.

I did this with my son's girlfriend years ago. I looked at her happy pictures and asked her what was going on when it was taken. She lit up like a Christmas tree to tell me. It was what she was genuinely happy about at that moment. I then pointed out other pictures that, although she was smiling, didn't reflect true happiness from the inside as the other pictures indicated. She saw what I saw then. There was a distinct difference.

I tried this with Agent 007 too! She sent me a selfie out by the pool while at her timeshare. I told her to save that picture as I had never seen her look so relaxed and happy. I asked her to look at that picture and then at herself in the mirror every day. If she didn't see that same happy reflection, she needed to change something.

So, dear reader, I challenge you to do it differently this year. Resolve to be happy and at peace. Rewrite those New Year's resolutions. Define what being at peace and being happy is for YOU, then do it! Set your soul free even if it is for only a few minutes at first. Strip down those big things on your list and look at them from the basics. Find your inner child that was content and happy to eat a PB&J and color. Marvel at the calm of sitting by water. Take a bubble bath, read that book, ride a bike, do a cartwheel, or build that model airplane. Make it a game if you have to. Your goal is to do *one thing* each day. Your angels will help lead you to more of those situations, circumstances or opportunities. They too, want to see you genuinely happy. When you light up with joy and happiness, it emanates to others and, if nothing else, it plants a seed by example for them to find their own internal happiness.

Just find ways to make *you* happy. Not everyone else. Celebrate every small milestone. Get excited over being just one step closer. Breathe. Believe. Listen to your soul. Look for moments to be happy and the happy will find YOU!

CHAPTER 24

DIVINE FEMININE LESSONS

I went to a reader named Dee. I just kept hearing that I was supposed to get a reading. I didn't understand why, but I literally found this woman's card in my car from someplace I had gone. I asked for a sign that I was supposed to go to this woman versus my woo-woo practice group for a message. The answer was this reader specifically. I scheduled an appointment with her and went over to her house.

When I sit down with a reader, I know what I want to hear and know about. Rarely though, do I tell them. I don't want to feed them any information or lead them. Do I get every bit of information I want back during the reading? Nope, not a lot. I get puzzle pieces. In the woo-woo world, we call them "seeds." Seeds that are planted to create further thought and help to get you off your soapbox. I had a very large soapbox—almost an island unto myself!

What she was directed to talk to me about was the divine feminine versus the divine masculine.

Now mind you, this stuff is all Greek to me. She proceeded to tell me that spirit wanted me to look up and research divine feminine women in history. Supposedly, there were things to know and learn about them. These were women who ruled countries. They were strong, beautiful and yet feminine. She dropped names like Cleopatra, Joan of Arc, Mother Mary, and Queen Victoria.

Not a fan of history stories, nor the homework spirit was assigning to me, all I heard was, blah blah blah, get out of my yoga pants and put on a skirt. OK, easy enough. The end. Right? NOPE.

She didn't agree with my solution of how to fix this as I most certainly was missing the point. I'm also sure she was probably annoyed at my reply. She responded that there was much more to learn from these great women.

(Insert bored eye roll here) All I heard and interpreted was I wasn't girly enough for a man and I needed to wear a dress. I told her that boys were yucky in my world right now and it wasn't important to me. I assured her that despite how I might look at that exact moment I was indeed girly. OK, I was most of the time. I admitted, I had been slacking off in the dressing-up department since moving. So, what! It wasn't like I was dating yet.

Seriously, why was spirit telling her to tell me this stuff? Hadn't I been through enough? There wasn't a straight answer to this. Only a puzzle piece. Honestly, I left thinking this reading was a huge waste of time. Spirit thought otherwise and would not let this subject go.

I honestly got frustrated for a bit over this topic. I don't know what life she'd been living, but there was no power in being a girl in the world I lived in. In my world I felt being a girl meant that you had to be subservient, bow down and give away your rights and power. Being a girl meant you give and rarely receive. That's all I knew.

So, what was this reader, Dee, talking about? I can honestly say it's taken more time than I care to admit to kind of get the purpose of this message. It's obviously more than just a skirt thing. I do, indeed, need more work in this area. OK, maybe a *lot* more. Hey, I can rock a pair of five-inch heels, a miniskirt, and get dolled up like the best of them, but does that mean I'm in my divine feminine power? No. This is what I needed to work on. It was not going to be a one-and-done fix either.

Now the question became if this was just my life or everyone else's too? This is what I allowed. This is what I felt I had to do. This is where boundary setting comes in. This behavior is not an equal exchange of energy.

I met my friend Cathy after the reading, and we had a massive discussion over this in the middle of a library. I can only imagine the looks we got from those overhearing me plead my case. I did not comprehend what the message was supposed to be about on this subject. I was supposed to figure it out and embrace the divine feminine versus the divine masculine.

A couple of friends and I are comparing notes about how we are getting better at setting boundaries and allowing things to be done for us on occasion without reciprocity. Being in your Divine feminine is about being powerful in *receiving*. You know, actually allowing someone to do something for *you*.

I mean, hey, let's start from the very beginning. Women are the portals for souls to come into this world. Now, this is not going to be a feminist girl-power type of thing but there is power in silence, power in being gentle and receiving. Have I mastered this yet? Not even close! Most men move too slowly for me.

I question if I was a guy in my past life. Why? The guys are the ones who seem to have all the power and are action oriented. Sadly, I seem to have this side of me down pat. Receiving? No so much!

I used to study the guys in my world. I knew what their games and tactics were. Everybody's got patterns and habits that give them away. Silently watch, and you'll find out! I should have been studying the girls and how they were in their divine feminine and received.

What I have been slowly understanding is that I attracted a lot of people in my life who *allow me to be and do masculine things and not receive anything in compensation.* I am oftentimes the boss in charge and putting other people's needs first.

I am not finger-pointing here. I own and accept the part I have played in this behavior. What I think Dee was trying to get across is that there is a different kind of power I had not yet learned to embrace.

Divine feminine powers receive, which is the yin energy. The *masculine powers do,* which is the yang energy. We all possess both sides. It is when you haven't mastered the balance of both, that it can become problematic.

Doing it my way has served me well in a lot of different ways but has not served me well in others. I have a lot to learn still. My balance in this department is way off and old habits die hard. Damn, some days I feel really messed up learning all of this! Jeez. Am I there yet? Nope! I seem to be aware of it more and more though and make corrections bit by bit.

I took the time to conjure up past scenarios to see where I went wrong and what it should have looked like. Well, for starters it is receiving compliments and just saying thank you. That's it. It's allowing someone to help you and do things for you without feeling obligated in return. There is power in allowing this.

I realized I have a lot of friends who have mastered the art of getting guys to do things for them. Like seriously, I thought they were selfish for having things taken care of for them. It was almost like they were lazy! I honestly felt bad for the guys! But then again, because I also was more in my divine masculine side, is that why they kept me around as a friend?

I'm sure I'm not the only one, but have you ever just seen somebody in a room, and they have such a presence and people simply do things hand-over-fist to give them whatever they want? People do things for them, and they have a "they rule the country" kind of attitude. They haven't said a word, raised a fist or their voice. They just are present, and they seem, sometimes, innocently powerful. They just receive. In my opinion that is the divine feminine.

I can honestly say that I am still a work in progress on this. Allowing someone to do something for me without feeling like I need to do fifty things to say thank you back is very, very hard. I grew up thinking it was supposed to be this way. I am realizing this has a lot to do with unspoken societal expectations and the women we model ourselves after in our lives. I can see this in my bloodline for sure.

It has taken a lot of time, effort and examples to see how the divine feminine actually works for me. This is all part of what I am learning about right now. Spirit continues to put situations and examples in front of me to observe. I am still learning and doing a lot of UN-learning.

Frankly, my issue is patience. I come from the mentality of "if I want something done, in the time frame I want it done in, I need to do it myself—and I will do it in my five-inch heels, thank you very much." THAT is the divine masculine side.

It's time to change the tape.

What I have also come to realize is that there are many men in my life right now who are OK with me being in more of a divine masculine state. I get things done. I jump in to help and do things without being asked. It's a much-needed break for a lot of them when I take care of things. They stand back and receive when I am around. It's not that they asked; I just thought it was expected of me. I have been allowing it. (My bad!) Guess what that is? They are embracing their divine feminine side by allowing me to take care of things as I was embracing my divine masculine side.

As these little lessons pop up, I am aware that this is all related to setting boundaries. The more I continue to make corrections, the more I feel it is another brick in my new foundation going forward for my future.

CHAPTER 25

DEATH DOULA

I learned a new term this past week! *DEATH DOULA.*

The Rhine Research Center at Duke University had a speaker this past week who discussed hospice work, death doulas, and mediumship. It was a fascinating combination! My friend Cathy, who does hospice work, invited me and I went.

I swear, I live under a rock sometimes! I had no idea what the word even meant, let alone that it existed prior to this event. So, if you also don't know, I hereby grace you with a good old Wikipedia explanation:

A death midwife, or death doula, is a person who assists in the dying process, much like a midwife or doula does with the birthing process. It is often a community-based role, aiming to help families cope with death through recognizing it as a natural and important part of life. The role can supplement and go beyond hospice. Practitioners perform a large variety of service, including but not limited to creating death plans, and providing spiritual, psychological, and social support before and just after death. Their role can also include more logistical activities, helping with services, planning funerals and memorial services, and guiding mourners in their rights and responsibilities.

The Rhine had guest speaker Debra Diamond come in to discuss and explain how she has tied all of this together in her experience. She has written two books on the subject, if you are interested.

It was truly fascinating, endearing, and validating. She stated that if the body is ready to go but the soul is not, the soul will hold out and death will not happen. If the soul is ready but the body has not shut down entirely yet, nothing will happen. It is only when the soul is ready and the body ceases at the same time that the soul transitions, leaving/discarding the earthly body. The body dies, but the soul lives on!

I also learned that while she is sitting with a loved one as a doula, the hospice patient *hears what you say*, even though it appears that they don't. (PSA: watch what you say!) She used the example of a lady walking into the hospice room, saying, "Is he dead yet?" (a little too excited) and the patient acknowledged to Debra that he heard it. With her being a medium, she has often had conversations with those who cannot speak for themselves.

Also fascinating was that despite the body lying there during the end of life not moving or responding, their *soul* is transitioning between two realms. The soul has moments when it leaves the body and visits loved ones, those who have already transitioned, who are waiting to receive them on the other side. There is no clock, so nobody knows exactly how long or how often they come and go. It has been said that Steve Jobs's sister reported on the day he died, he uttered, "OH WOW. OH WOW. OH WOW." I guess he got the chance to see a highlight reel before he officially transitioned!

When my dear grandma was at the hospital a few years ago, not doing well, my mother sat with her. Mom mentioned that at one point, grandma suddenly opened her eyes and smiled. My mother realized that grandma was looking past her but looked *so happy*! Mom asked grandma what she was looking at. My grandma said that my grandfather (who had passed away many years earlier) was right behind my mother. He was there with other family to let her know that they were there when she was ready to go. My mom said she turned to look behind her and saw no one. My grandmother closed her eyes and passed away soon after.

My mother was an RN before she retired and very "left-brain" oriented. If it was not documented in a book as fact, you were "making it up" and it was "all in your head." I think it took a lot of courage for my mom to tell me about this instance, considering it was a contradiction to everything she preached to me growing up.

Trying to comfort Mom, I validated what she said. I truly believed that grandpa did come to let grandma know that he was there, and she would be in great hands once she was ready to go. I feel it was helpful for my left-brained mother to hear that "*she*" was not making this up. (But oh, the temptation to channel my adolescence and throw back some of the words she always told me!) Mom wrote out what happened and hesitantly shared it with my aunts and uncles. She had my full support. To her surprise, no one questioned her about it either.

My point in sharing this story was that hearing Debra speak only further confirmed the experiences I have had so far in my life and my personal work so far as a medium helping people to speak with their loved ones who have crossed.

Cathy and I did a lot of head-bobbin' in acknowledgment throughout the talk Debra gave. I also learned that Cathy had actually taken one or two doula classes, which I did not know. She is so awesome!

In the big scheme of things, the talk was fascinating on many different levels. It truly warmed my heart that the soul sneaks in and out of this realm, despite what the body is doing. It's free even if only for a few moments before it transitions for good.

I give sincere appreciation to all the doulas and hospice workers out there. They give family and friends a much-needed break so that their loved ones are never without someone by their side. I had no idea they even existed prior to this event. Death doulas are a special kind of earth angel along with all the hospice workers out there. They should just walk around with wings on, for all to see and admire as they still walk on the earth.

If you feel called to do such work, there are many training facilities to help you know how and what you can do to be of service. Please look them up. Many need you.

CHAPTER 26

WHAT'S UP, DOC?

Occasionally, I get nudges to give someone a reading. I feel compelled to at least offer and if that person is open, I will spend time with them relaying the information that is meant for them.

I have a friend and coworker, Mary. She is by far one of the sweetest and most caring people I have met in a long time. The more I learn about her, the more I am in awe. In business, Mary and I work well together in real estate as our outlook and philosophy are aligned as to how we handle things and treat people. She has been an angel for me since moving to North Carolina. Today, she told me I was an angel for her, and there was a reason I was put in her life.

For a while now, I have been getting nudges to give her a reading. The timing hadn't been right between our schedules, up until recently. I was sick when I came back from England, but finally started to feel better. I again got a nudge to speak to her. Someone on the other side was anxious to give her a message. We arranged to speak over the phone.

I was able to bring through a gentleman who meant the world to her and wanted to speak through me. After giving her all of the evidence, I had been given, she validated everything and then told me her story. Their love story.

This was the love of her life. She called him "DOC," because of his profession. Everything in their lives clicked. When he fell ill and passed away, a part of her died as well. Their happily-ever-after was cut short. Through the love they shared, Doc would now and forever be the benchmark relationship for which she would gauge future relationships. It was understandably gut-wrenching for her.

During our conversation, I told her that he is still around, you just can't see him. You see, your loved ones will show you a sign if you don't already have one assigned for them. For many, butterflies, pennies, feathers, rainbows, and birds are the sign. If they show up in your path, you know it is from your loved one. Mary had not heard about asking for a sign. So, I explained that Doc would be willing to prove to her that he is, indeed, around and watching over her. He would show her a sign if she asked him to.

We then chatted about what signs were and how they can show up as either a word or a picture. Also, how to make the sign you choose unique. For example, don't ask to be shown a red rose around Valentine's Day. That is way too coincidental. I encouraged her to ask for a sign that, if presented or shown, there would be no question that it was from him. I also suggested that she create a deadline. She said she would do this.

Not much later, I had the urge to reach out to her to discuss a business deal we had going on together. After the business conversation, she said, "I have to tell you something."

She told me that after our conversation, she asked Doc that if he was around her, could he show her a *pink bunny* in a word or picture before midnight on Thursday. She then told me she looked everywhere for the sign. She looked at T-shirts, commercials, social media, and listened to the words people spoke. No one said anything, nor did she see a *"pink bunny."* She was losing hope. She wondered if maybe he wasn't around.

She had gone to bed as usual on Thursday not yet having seen the sign she asked for. Suddenly, something woke her up out of a dead sleep. She bolted upright and looked around to see what the possible disruption was. Her dog slept peacefully on its back, not disturbed at all. She got up to look out the window and see if there was a noise or disturbance. She saw nothing. Fully awake now, she turned on the television to hopefully help her get sleepy again. She joked that since she was up, she might as well turn on the Hallmark Channel!

Then, a commercial came on with the *Energizer Bunny*. She stared at it—staring back at her was, a *pink bunny*! She said she had never seen this commercial at all, ever. Then, the bunny walked off the screen, stuck its head back onto the screen and winked at her. She said she sat there in awe! She then asked herself if that just happened.

She admitted that it freaked her out a little bit. She was, indeed, fully awake! Then, she had a feeling come over her that Doc was with her, sending her his love and that was the sign from him! He proved to her that he really was there watching over her, he heard her request, and gifted her the sign she requested—even if he had to wake her up to show her.

When she told me this story, I had wave after wave of goose bumps—which is my confirmation sign! It was as if Doc was also with me again saying, "thank you for helping!" I was truly grateful!

Mary told me that for the first time since Doc died more than two years prior, she finally felt at peace. She knows now that he is around her still. She feels comforted in a way that she hasn't been able to feel since he passed. She thanked me for helping her get to that place.

Personally, my cheeks hurt from smiling so much. I was so happy and just wanted to share.

I had to laugh—as we ended the conversation, she said, "*You can't make this shit up!*" I couldn't agree more.

CHAPTER 27

WHAT DO YOUR NUMBERS SAY

Anyone remember talking pig Latin? You remember, that once-upon-a-time covert language you spoke with your friends so adults around you didn't know what you were saying?

If you don't know, or don't remember, here's how you do it: Drop the first letter of any word, add it to the end of the word, then add "AY." So, for example: *chicken soup* would be *hickencay oupsay*. Frankly, at the time, it took very little effort to do it, but it allowed you to get away with saying things around your parents. Today, being out of practice, it feels like a long-lost language from ancient history!

Now? I speak numbers. Numbers and combinations of numbers truly can tell you, at the least, some basics to help you on your journey. Numbers are everywhere. These are the repetitive numbers you see on license plates, clocks, televisions, phones, calendars, and numerous other areas just ripe for seeing.

Number-speak started during my awakening period. It drove me nuts, too! It started when I was in a spell of grief and despair over events going on in my life. I kept seeing a certain time on the clock.

I also kept seeing this same set of numbers so suddenly, and so repetitively, that I could not, *not*, pay attention any longer. That started me questioning the meaning of these numbers. I finally figured out that one sequence of numbers was my great-aunt's birthday and that she must be around. That gave me comfort. Every time I saw these numbers, I would just say "hi" to her.

So then, we were on to a new set of numbers. "911." Let me tell you, this freaked-me the hell out!

We are programmed here in the States to dial 911 for help. It also was a reminder of the tragic events of 9/11! If that were the case, why were my angels showing me 911? Like, seriously, what could I do on an earthly plane to help them in the spiritual plane?

Honestly it made me question if it was a warning of things to come. "*Emergency going to happen—warning—911!*"

I truly tried my darnedest to ignore that number. True to fashion, the more I try to ignore something they want me to know, the more they make *sure* I see it. They don't seem to mind that it is irritating the pants off of me. Once I get it through my thick head, my angels and guides will lay off. Anyway, during my divorce, my grandmother passed away. Even being in a completely different state for her funeral, they still showed me 911 repetitively. IT-WOULD-NOT-STOP.

Ever just hit the wall? I already somewhat was at that point. I had no energy to figure out on my own what 911 meant. My heart and soul were hurting upside down, backward and all day on Sunday. All I knew in my world was that the number was not a good sign. I was grateful for the warning but was just too tired on every level, and in every way, to figure it out on my own. I felt my choice, at the time if asked, was to walk in front of the proverbial bus and just get it over with. Just hit me with whatever this emergency was and be done!

I ended up having a reading after I got back from the funeral. Believe it or not, the message was that the number, for me, was not a bad thing. I am sure the person reading for me could feel the panic in my energy regarding the number as I sat there. Relieved but still slightly hesitant, I tried to think more positively about the number's meaning but needed more information.

With the slightest amount of relief lifted off my shoulders, I was led to do further research on number 911. In doing so, I started looking at other combinations and the meanings of those numbers. There were other sets of repeating numbers that I was aware of that suddenly spoke a message to me. They were not as scary as 911 was to me at the time but, alas, I was now learning a new language of numerology or, as I coined how I look at things—number-speak.

I was also counseled to discuss with my angelic team what I want a number sequence to mean. Not what anyone else wanted it to be but what it would mean to MOI.

At first, I didn't realize I had a choice. Oh, but we do! Angels really want to work with you. It's a personal language just between you and them. It is meant to help you receive messages. I was now on a quest. What do I want these numbers to mean to me versus what do different people on the Internet say? I researched for ideas to formulate my personal number assignments.

Obviously, there are an infinite amount of number combinations out there. I started out with the basic numbers of one through ten, in sets of three or more. I also gave thought to what number sets I continually saw and resorted to checking out others' opinions online. That led me to create and adopt my own meanings. Just like in my signs book I filled out before going overseas, I now had meanings for numbers.

Once I had some of the basics down, I had a talk during my prayer time to let my angels know that if they put certain numbers in front of me, I would accept them to mean certain things. I also reminded them that I don't like massive changes to hit me upside the head, so if they could just warn me ahead of time (555) I would greatly appreciate their cooperation.

So now, I have this little angel-number language going! It's certainly not like sitting down with a cup of tea and chatting, but it has been very helpful! It's like reading basic statements translated from numbers. This was at least a step forward! Now, we're talking!

My nemesis is by far, number 555. I truly have a love-hate relationship with that number. The number 555 is my number that change is coming! Ugh, it presents to me well in advance of upcoming changes (again, because I requested it). Sometimes it has been so overtly put in my face that I wondered if a house was going to drop out of the sky!

Does 555 always mean something bad? No! Do I always think of it as bad at first? Yes! (I'm being honest here!) Do I like changes? As long as it is me making them on my terms, then yes! Do I get that kind of control—Hell, no!

Another number that I am having a hard time with is 222. You see, I gave 222 the definition of "go with the flow." For my fellow scuba diving friends, it also means DRIFT DIVE.

For those who don't scuba, there is an underwater current that will literally just take you along for a ride. You can swim against it, but you ultimately will still go wherever it takes you. So basically, just go with the flow and relax. It's going to take you forward whether or not you want to. I have a hard time with this number for many reasons. What does go with the flow mean? I have *no clue* a lot of the time. Undoubtedly, I overthink this number more than any other.

Combinations of number sequences have also been a factor I had to consider. Over the course of the last few years, I have learned that if my great-aunt's birthday shows up along with 555, it's a warning to me that some change is going to come about, and it's going to scare me or make me feel uncomfortable, but *she is with me*. For that, I am grateful! Knock on wood, for a long time now, that combination hasn't happened!

The *trifecta* is when my aunt's birthday shows up with 555 and 222. Trust me, I am grateful to know ahead of time and be warned. At times, I have wanted to go hide in a dark closet until "whatever-is-going-to-happen" passes. This has only happened a few times thus far.

The standard repetitive saying I keep hearing from my channeled readings for myself is, "*Get comfortable with being uncomfortable.*" It is so much easier said than done. I get uncomfortable with 555 a *lot*. Is it repetitively bad? Again, Nope! In fact, a lot of times it is great! Truly an optimist at heart, my pessimistic side makes me think of the worst case just so I am prepared. Gratefully, though, when I see my other numbers come up and knowing what they mean, I know I will be fine.

Number-speak to me is like angel text messaging with quick bursts of information to be aware of. I don't have to think much about what they mean anymore.

Like any language, the more you use it, the more fluent you get. I see the number, know the message, and then must wait to see what it pertains to. Should a new number combination arise, I will assign it a new meaning based on what is going on in my life.

To my fellow readers, I encourage you to work with your own set of numbers and assign meanings for your own reference. Then, see what messages you get. It can't be as scary as 911—which, by the way, to me means: *Be The Example*, not the emergency.

Chapter 28

Hello! Is This Thing On?

My friend Angie has been having a pretty rough go of it of late. I am privy to a lot, but not all, of what she has on her plate. Spirit nudged me to ask a friend to give her a reading. So, I arranged for someone from my practice group, Sam, to do a reading for her. My friend Sam is *AH-MAZ-ING* at receiving channeled messages.

I don't personally read for Angie or even friends I talk to often because of what I know. Angie deserved a reader who had zero background knowledge about her and her stresses. I felt the messages I might receive for her could be colored because of my prior knowledge of her. So, I handed the torch to Sam as a favor to me. Sam read and gifted her information from spirit that she needed to hear. Angie was very grateful!

Two days later, Angie and I hung out with a few other friends to chat, which ran into the early evening. (You know how we women can talk!) So, after we said our goodbyes, Angie and I opted to grab a bite and chat further. We bantered with the waiter, ingested libations, and ate pizza. This led to me dripping sauce on my white shirt—

seriously, what is the magnetic attraction of pizza sauce to a white shirt? *sigh* I digress. Anyway, we continued to chat on the car ride back to my place. She turned off the car while we chatted in the parking lot.

I was having a soapbox moment about how I think things should be done versus what spirit wants done. Don't even get me started on the timing of events! Surprised? HA! Spirit versus my ego—who do YOU place your bets on? Despite what I know, I still have moments when I tend to push back on the way things are done. Anyway, toward the end of my rant, I literally threw my hands up in the air and explained that I surrender to whatever spirit wants!

Just then, the radio in her car lit up, turning on despite her engine being off for a while. We both looked at it and heard very clearly the words "WE ARE GRATEFUL"—and then it turned back off, again.

If it weren't for well-padded thighs from eating pizza, dead serious, my jaw would have hit the floorboard. We both were extremely wide-eyed in awe. Our mouths gaped open in complete shock. I looked at her and said, "Did that really just happen? You saw that, right? You heard that, too?" Just as wide-eyed and in awe herself, she confirmed that she did indeed see exactly what I saw and heard! Spirit, being all around us, used the radio at the exact moment and wanted to be part of the conversation to show gratitude.

We both burst out laughing! I was hooting, you can't make this shit up! Holy cow!

Despite me paying attention most of the time, I am still in shock and awe of all the cool things that happen like it was the first time! I hope I never lose my inner five-year-old wonder and amazement! Think they will slip me the lottery numbers?

Dear reader,

Please know that spirit finds a way to make sure you get messages whether you want to or are ready to hear them. Spirits are always with you. Songs on the radio, billboards, license plates, opening books to see an exact phrase, and even a well-timed phone call from someone are just some of the many examples of the ways you can receive a message from spirit. They truly are giving you messages all-the-time. Just be aware!

CHAPTER 29

GETTING "THE BIRD"

Yup! I am getting "the bird" a lot these days! Is it good? Is it bad? Trust me, I want to know, too!

I have created certain signs that represent certain messages. Remember, in my world, 222 is drift, dive, or go with the flow, while 555 means changes are coming! My birthday is my great-aunt's, so I look for that number. The dragonfly is my grandmother, and the red cardinal is my grandfather.

So, let's just cut to the chase. A red cardinal represents my grandpa. *The end.* Right? Well, if all he did was show up or fly by like he has done in the past, I would say, "Yes!" Is that what is happening? No! The erratic behavior of "Grandpa," now has me scrambling to figure out bird morse code. Let me explain.

I have birdseed out on my patio for all sorts of birds. I am used to seeing them come and go. The cardinal though, not as much. When I do see the cardinal, I am pretty happy. I don't take it for granted. Yes, it is the state bird of North Carolina, but I don't control where they fly or make appearances. Anyway, I hear the chirp associated with the cardinal and look out the French door. There is, indeed, a cardinal.

"Hi, grandpa!"

The odd thing that happened though, is that the cardinal flew to the windowpane and tapped on it, then flapped its wings repeating this same feat of tapping, then flapping its wings over and over again. I was so in *awe* that I videotaped it for my group of woo-woo friends! What the heck does tapping from a cardinal mean and, if it's my grandpa, what is he saying?

Does anyone know bird morse code? Anyone? The cardinal flies away after doing this for about two minutes, then comes back and does it *again*. This happened a total of five times. Not at any specific interval, either.

OK, let's just call a spade a spade, here. When the same bird knocks on the window, it's a big deal! Well, it is to me. This is my sign from my grandfather. The question is, what is he trying to tell me with the taps? Some of it included frantically flapping his wings.

Is it a warning? A message of the arrival of someone I didn't want to see? A heads-up about something? Maybe a message to get outside and do something. Hopefully, it is about someone coming to give me a check for a million dollars! Good, bad, or indifferent, I am just not sure. Seriously, no clue. Maybe he wanted to come in and take a bath? Hang out with me while I worked? I had no idea at all. All I did know was that grandpa was making a pretty big production for my benefit!

I asked my mom her thoughts. She thought maybe the cardinal was seeing his reflection and wanted to come in because it was cold?

OK, interesting theory! So, I went outside. I saw *zero* reflection at all based on how the sun was positioned. I even added more birdseed, thinking that maybe he was hungry. I still had no explanation.

Well, "grandpa" came back repeating this pattern off and on for about a week. Something was definitely up. I decided to turn to Google for further explanation.

The cardinal totem and spirit animal information states to listen to my intuition. The cardinal is often associated with people who get out there and get things done. The symbolism says to be very clear about what you want and your intentions. Also, to set clear and insightful goals. It also warns you to be careful of your thoughts and what you are manifesting yet gives permission to start those projects you have wanted to accomplish.

I agree with all of it. The question is, why the urgency of the cardinal repeatedly coming to my same window over and over again? I still feel that the franticness and frequency mean something. I decided to be exceptionally clear about the bottom line of what I want.

AHEM! HEAR YE, HEAR YE: I want to continue to be happy with no drama. Elevate my internal peace even more. I want to see signs and signals with clarity for my chosen path.

Seriously, I was in shock at all the super clear things that I stated. Where did *that* come from? My motto for the year was *"my voice, my vision."* I stated the facts. At this moment, I feel great!

Grandpa is still visiting. He is truly adorable in what he is doing.

I am grateful for whatever messages he is trying to give me.

I'm paying super close attention to my dreams and any messages I receive. I even went back and read a lot of my channeled messages and got further clarity on a few things. Maybe, that was the message! Regardless, when Mother Nature makes such a profound presence in my life, I pay attention to what I feel, see, and what is going on in my life. It most certainly is a piece of a puzzle I cannot ignore!

CHAPTER 30

SURPRISE!

Despite it being the first Mercury retrograde of the year, I had a surprising number of really cool little things that happened. I heard words like "master manifester" used a lot about myself. I also heard the words "get out of your own way" (sadly, a *lot*) so things can happen. I have a hard time balancing those two statements. Honestly, more than I am willing to admit.

I experienced a run of manifestations that had been happening way too often to be coincidental. Spirit had my attention at this. For example, despite being "good" and eating healthier, I wanted a donut a few weeks ago. I just had a taste for one! I wasn't trying to deny myself but more like curtail the desire. I survived the drive into the office—past the local donut shop. (phew) I put my stuff down in my office and headed to the kitchen to get a cup of coffee. Wouldn't you know it? There were not one, but two boxes of donuts on the table free for grabbing! Now, I'm not going to look a gift horse in the mouth—yes, I indulged in (only) one donut.

Next, I happened to be staring out the window looking at the scenery and it suddenly flashed in my head that I had not seen the cardinal that had been pecking at my window in two days. Within five minutes, there was the cardinal at my window, flapping its wings again. Well, *that* was easy! Wait, did I do that or was it a coincidence?

Then, I *really* didn't want to attend this new agent class I was in. It was redundant information about real estate I already knew but it was "mandatory" for the new company I was working for. I knew the subject matter like the back of my hand and could have *taught* the class. Knowing my experience, they asked me not to "overly share" so as not to confuse the other students. Lo and behold, I literally got sick and couldn't go. Humor me, it did get me out of class!

My point is that these little "trinkets" of surprise out of a grab bag that belongs to spirit were at every turn for me. I tried to wrap my head around this. Am I doing it? It was happening far too much to be a coincidence! I started paying attention to what in tarnation exactly am I doing?

I realized I would see or think of something that I wanted. Then, as fast as the thought flew in, it flew out. (Serious squirrel brain.) Those thoughts were replaced by other thoughts and deadlines! In theory, I was acknowledging what I wanted, and then "letting it go." Honestly, I wasn't hanging my hat on ANY-THING! I think what I have been doing is just sending it out to the universe inadvertently. I thought about my kids—they would suddenly text me. I needed a solution to a problem—it was practically dropped into my lap. This has happened so much that I am more aware of it and paying so much more attention to it.

Now, I'm sure I could say that what you think about you bring about. Also, being psychic, did I make something happen or just know it ahead of time? I didn't know!

It was time for a "counsel meeting" with my angels. Usually, I whine about something, and they listen. I want you to know that, despite my faith, I still get scared and worried about things at times. I am human! So along with that, I still attempt to "lay the law down so things go how I think they should go." (Trust me, I hear them laughing at me.) Does it happen my way? Nah. Sometimes it's a true compromise. Like, for example, I was having a "moment" about my resources and how much better I would feel if I just had a larger amount than what I had. I realize that my anxiousness is about the future. About tomorrow. The tomorrow that hasn't happened yet.

It's so much easier to tell you all those funny quips about worry than to apply it to myself. Trust me, I get it! My favorite one is "*Worry is like a rocking chair: It gives you something to do but never gets you anywhere.*" Or another favorite I remind myself of is, "*A mortgage company will give you a loan based on the fact that you promise to pay them back every month, and they don't know if you will be employed tomorrow.*" So, what I gather from all this is that I need to worry about tomorrow, well, tomorrow.

So, during a conversation with a friend, I relayed an idea to them to implement. They called me out, asking if it was such a great idea, why was *I* not doing it? (Insert cartoon light bulb over my head!) Then, I got another call from a friend who asked me to do some side work for pay. I swear I could see my angels' smirk in my mind's eye.

Ask and you shall receive.

You see, I asked for additional resources because I would feel better if there were more. Although they didn't drop money into my account, my angels gave me *opportunities to make money*. They even lined it up. I spoke out loud to spirit and said to them, "*You are all sneaky!*" The saying they put back into my head was that you can lead a horse to water, but you can't make them drink. So drink! Ugh! Message received. I can't whine if they keep giving me opportunities, right?

Another thing that manifested for me then was a plant. I thought about how a nice, large, artificial potted plant would look in my new office and figured if I saw one while I was out, I should get it. Within five days, I had one that was given to me for free! It was exactly what I had in mind!

While having coffee recently at our favorite Barnes and Noble, a friend and I experienced one of the coolest things. After a few hours of chatting, she excused herself to go to the bathroom and came back with a book called *Heal*. I just stared at her in awe. I asked her why she picked up that book. She said it just caught her eye! She said, "*We should both read it.*"

She then got up and went back to the shelf and saw a second copy of the book and grabbed it as it was the last one. She literally walked straight to the counter and paid for them immediately, then handed me one. It happened that fast.

We had never discussed this book or how I even knew of it. Trust me, I thanked her! It was the written supplement to the Netflix documentary, also called *Heal*. Another one of my friends randomly mentioned it to me about a month ago, recommending that I should watch it. I couldn't find it on Netflix for some reason and thus forgot about it. So, when my friend I was sitting with having coffee randomly picked up that book without discussion or prompting and brought it back to where we were seated, I could only shake my head in wonderment. Out of thousands of books in that store and no discussion on the topic at all she buys it for me. I cannot make this up! Spirit works in mysterious ways!

At my office I got a text from my mom sending me a picture of my favorite great-aunt that she suddenly came across. I just got the feeling that it was my great-aunt's way of saying hi to me and that she is with me helping in whatever ways that she can.

Driving home one afternoon I realized I hadn't seen a deer in a long time. I turned the corner and there stood a deer on the side of the road.

On a completely different subject, the Halls lozenges I have been eating have pep talks on the wrappers—spoken straight to my heart from the great beyond!

Maybe it has steadily happened, and I just haven't paid attention to it. We all have moments when we feel streaks of luck are on our side. Just a lot of events recently have certainly caught my attention! I am not going to look a gift horse in the mouth or take anything for granted. I'm forever saying thank you out loud to my angels and sincerely mean it!

I want to stress that not everything goes my way. I don't want to imply that. I still have small lessons to learn and hurdles to overcome. I am just eternally grateful for all the things that do happen.

I know that I am being looked after by angels and guides and they are lining things up for me to be aware of. I am enjoying them pointing these events out for me to see and appreciate. Trust me, they add up and I couldn't be more grateful!

CHAPTER 31

TELL HER! TELL HER!

I currently work in the real estate industry and feel I may be phasing out of it in the near future. This is my truer calling. Alas, the old is familiar and easy. True to my inner five-year-old, I will probably have to go kicking and screaming. Ultimately, I know that it's getting close to cutting the cord. It's these other moments that show me how much good I can still do for others, often in ways I don't even understand at the moment. I love how I feel when I help people. It does my soul good!

I've worked with people all my life. I realize I have consistently just known things without being able to identify exactly *how* I know. It has happened all throughout my career and helped me in many ways even though I didn't know it at the time. It most definitely has gotten stronger as time has gone on!

To my detriment, and my advantage, I have tried to make myself available to my clients anytime they had questions or concerns. This has been an ongoing lesson on boundaries for me. There are some habits I still can't let go of. So, I want to tell you about Tammy.

Tammy and her husband Jim (married forty-two years) have been clients of mine for what seems a thousand years. They had a unique balance. Jim was the ideas person and Tammy looked after the business side. They played hard and worked harder. They lived on the water, had a boat, cool cars, and constantly had a new project on the horizon. So, at one of their play moments, Jim flew up to go hang out with some friends on Lake Erie and go sailing with the guys. Tammy stayed back. At the time, I was in Missouri for my grandmother's ninetieth birthday celebration.

Out of the blue, I got a call from a mutual friend about Tammy and Jim. There had been an accident. Jim had been knocked overboard and drowned. Tammy was understandably devastated. The mutual friend wanted me to know in case she called. I was in complete shock.

To this day, Tammy still has moments of intense grief. She tries to get along in life but has moments when the world does not sit right on its axis, and she gets frustrated and confused. That's where I come in—and so did Jim.

Tammy called me in one of her frazzled states, asking where some paperwork was that she needed. I had nothing to do with any of this paperwork, but I answered her call and tried to help. I knew that my answers and familiar voice helped to calm her down. If I had anything to do with it, no one was going to take advantage of her.

As Tammy was talking to me, suddenly my third eye lit up and in my mind's eye, I kept seeing this arm *swiping* over top of her body. It happened over and over again. *Swipe! Swipe!* (Visualize an entire arm that suddenly clears all the smoke and fog out of a room except it was over and around Tammy). That's what it was like despite her being in another state from me. I kept seeing this action over and over and over again. At the time, I had *no clue* what was going on, but I continued to help Tammy on the phone and give her guidance. While I was talking to her, I then heard the words, "*Clear! Clear!*"

I got off the phone, and my heart went out to her. I suddenly had the urge to call her back. It was a very strong urge! I realized Jim was reaching through to ask me to help her. It was Jim saying *clear!* It was Jim doing the swiping above her head. He was putting the visual of her in my mind's eye. He wanted me to be his microphone to help her.

I truly was scared for a moment! This is not the capacity at which I operate in my career. Tammy doesn't know this side of me at all and now I need to merge the two sides of me? Oh boy. Talk about being a bit freaked out! It was just such an overwhelming feeling to help and give her his message! I called a friend and explained what had just happened and she said, "You need to call her right back, right now!" So, I did. *This* was definitely going to be an interesting call for sure!

I called Tammy back and explained that I have some "gifts." I explained that I believed Jim was trying to give her a message and would she be open to receiving it? I truly don't think I got the words fully out of my mouth before she loudly exclaimed, "Yes!" That's all it took. The floodgates opened, and I explained what I saw, felt, and what I knew Jim wanted her to know.

Jim wanted her to know that he wanted to "swipe" away the bad feelings she was having. Through me, he exclaimed that she had oppressive heaviness all around her and he needed to swipe it away and make it clear! She needed to take the constant burdens of the court cases against the boat's owner, the grief, and all the changes she had going on and just put them aside and clear her head! He kept saying, "I am trying to talk to you, but you can't hear me!"

Once she heard that, it was as if a light switch flipped for her. Suddenly, not frantic any longer, she seemed to come back to a state of awareness. It was as if those words penetrated the veil of sadness, and she heard him loud and clear. She said she felt he was giving her signs, but she did not know. for sure I assured her that he was, indeed, giving her signs but she must clear away everything so she can see with clear eyes.

He wanted her to go to the edge of the water, let the saltwater wash over her feet. He needed her to put the alcohol away. She needed to clear her head, just breathe, and honor her feelings instead of masking them. Then, she would hear him. He would be with her.

She absolutely and completely understood everything I was repeating to her! Through tears, she said she would do what he asked, and she suddenly didn't feel so out of control. She wanted to find her footing again.

She had some questions that Jim gave me answers to for her (like wondering if he was with their dog). I also had a sense of ease and peace that came over me as I conveyed the messages that he offered. More importantly, she also calmed down enough to think straight. Jim had, from the other side, taken charge like he had in life and laid out a game plan that made complete and perfect sense to her.

Through me, he spoke the words she would understand and listen to.

She thanked me over and over again before we hung up. I was just as grateful that she was open to receiving messages! Jim flooded me with a sense of appreciation for being able to help her with wave after wave of goose bumps.

I was in complete awe when I finished that call. The entire process, although not about me, felt amazing. I was so honored that Jim shoved his way through to direct me on how to help her. He made sure I knew it was him reaching through and found a way to ease her burdens.

Tammy still has moments, but they are much fewer and far between. She is slowly making her way back to doing a few fun things and has even tried dating. I speak to her off and on and am grateful to hear the slow return of the person she once was. No doubt, Jim is still helping to guide and direct her. It's another reminder that angels are all around us!

CHAPTER 32

NIGHT SHIFT ANGEL MESSENGERS & CATCHING YOUR DREAMS

I have days where I wake up tired from sleeping! Who knew? My active brain does not shut down. When I sleep, I dream. In fact, I dream a lot. So much so that I feel I am a walking storybook when the alarm goes off!

I never paid much attention to my dreams in the past other than to relay some funny part. Then, I realized certain things happened that seem to coincide with what was going on in my waking moments. Ever have a déjà vu moment? That is the feeling like you have done this before. Chances are, you have, *in-a-dream*. It was happening to me a lot! So, I started really paying attention. Game on!

Have you ever had a very profound dream? You know, the ones you will never forget. Something about the dream really sticks out. On occasion, I do. Many years ago (before I was even aware of all of this woo-woo stuff officially), I had a dream that my youngest son fell off a roof. *Scared the crap out of me!* I saw the house; I saw what side of the roof he was on and all I could do was watch from the end of a really long driveway. (I was an observer.) As a mother, it was not something I wanted to see. I felt helpless. So fast forward to today. Guess what he does right now while in college? *Works on roofs!* Think that doesn't scare the bejesus out of me? It does, *every single day.* I told him of this dream years ago and he remembers it to this day. (Yes, make Momma happy and be extra careful, baby!)

Never mind the interesting/concerning stuff. There is also the fun stuff! Dreams so wild, you doubt anyone could even make up such fabrications! Goodness, Hollywood should be so lucky to hear what goes on in my dreams sometimes! I feel some of my stories should come with warning labels and disclaimers!

How long is a dream? Some seem really short, don't they? Yet, others seem never-ending. I have had a few that I was not fond of. I basically said, "*peace out,*" and woke myself up. Whatever was going on, I didn't want to handle it, or it was unpleasantly dragging on. I made an "executive dream" decision and said, nope, not doing this!

In doing so, I learned (which may have been the point?) that I have more control to dictate the events in a dream or that I can work through the events presented to me. Do I remember this when asleep? Nope! I have a sleep app on my watch. It tracks my heart rate, marks when I am lightly sleeping, and when I am in a deep REM sleep—aka "dreaming." It is fascinating to me to see that I was only asleep for fifteen to twenty minutes but did so much in my dream!

Of course, I resort to the Internet and various dream books to help make sense of the symbols and events I recall. It is faster, at times, for quick reference or when I don't want to think or analyze. (I'm sure there is some twelve-step group for someone who doesn't want to overanalyze for five minutes!)

On rare occasions, the explanations I read make sense, but remember, the person writing it is basing it on their own life experiences and interpretation, not yours. So, for that reason, find the one that resonates best for you. I have yet to find that one-stop "go-to" place for constant reference. Again, I look but I take it with a grain of salt.

Prompted by some reading over the years, I realized some really cool stuff about my dreams! Why? Because I was on a quest to find out! (You can too!)

Dear reader, here's your homework! Before you go to sleep, make it your intent to find out the answers to these questions:

* Do you dream in color or black and white?

* Are you an observer of your dream or a participant?

* Have you ever seen yourself in a mirror in a dream?

* Have you ever had an experience that felt so real it was like you were awake only to have your alarm go off and realize you were asleep?

* Have you ever flown in the air or swam under water?

* Have you been aware that you're having a dream in the dream?

* How about going back into a (hopefully) good dream (wink wink, nudge nudge) after you got up to use the bathroom?

Again, if you want to know the answers to these questions, set your intention before you go to sleep that you want to know. Lucid dreaming is wild information!

So, let's assume you have the answers to some of these questions. Cool! You get a star for paying attention to those details! Woo-hoo!

What about the bad dreams, like falling, running through the woods naked, and being in a house on fire? I can honestly say that I have not had or been plagued with bad dreams like some have. (Knocking on wood as we speak!)

I have learned to pay attention to the storylines and symbolic messages in the dreams and try and piece them together. Not everything is literal but more often metaphorical in nature. These are probably the ones you need to call your friends in for a consultation of the meaning. I admit it can, at times, be like the game of *Clue* to figure out! (Colonel Mustard did it in the conservatory with the candlestick!) Rest assured, there is a meaning or a message in it.

Visitations: We need to talk about visitations from those who have crossed over. It is them! Talk to them if you can. Many times, they just want to give you a message of love and support you might not be aware of in your conscious state. When you are sleeping, your ego is out of the way, and you will be more receptive. Say hi or think about how you feel while with them in the dream.

What was that dream again? In my own personal dream recording, I have discovered that infusing my lungs with oxygen in the short distance from the bed to the potty is enough to make me forget. Yup, my brain will "delete, delete, delete." Therefore, I have trained myself to speak out loud the word, picture, or theme the minute I wake up until I can record my recollection in some way. As fast as a dream may appear it can also DIS-appear. So, how you record your dream is up to you. I wrote a song lyric, phrase, or word on a whiteboard at 2:48 a.m. and gone back to bed.

If it's a story-dream, personally, I talk way faster than I write. Therefore, for me, the effort to get pen, paper, turn on a light, prop the pillows up and then try and write, well, by then the dream is mostly gone. I have met a few people that this works for. So do what's best for you!

For me, at first, I bought one of those little recorder devices. Unfortunately, that required one more electronic device to be accountable for. No, no, and oh yeah, *no*! Frankly, I'm trying to be less plugged into electronic devices and more plugged into life! My latest trick for recording said crazy-night-movies, is to talk an email to myself on my phone, hit send, and go back to sleep. This works even if you must whisper! (If your significant other catches you, just tell them you are asking Jake at State Farm what he is wearing! LOL.) This not only saves it but also gives a time and date stamp.

I am now the proud owner of a book of night stories. I print them off and put them in a notebook. With the time and date stamp on them I find, interestingly, they are mostly recorded between 2 a.m. and 5 a.m.! How 'bout that? Eh?

Some of you swear you don't dream—well, I hate to say it, but you do. You're just not remembering them.

How can you remember? Ask! Before you go to bed, just say out loud or silently that it is your intention that you will remember your dreams or the key components and symbols as you are waking up.

Also ask your angels to make them clear, so you remember them! That way when you wake up, something should stand out.

Here's the big part. No matter how obscure the thought or image is, write it down or record it. You don't even have to know what it is! ("It looked/seemed/felt like [blank].") Put it off to the side. You don't have to analyze it until you are ready. Trust me, if you don't record it, it will evaporate into thin air. To enhance the opportunity, some people will put a crystal under their pillow or by their bed. Four that help are amethyst, quartz, hemimorphite, and Herkimer diamond. You can find these at your local metaphysical shop.

What the heck do all these story-images-signs in a dream mean? Well, I decided to go to a few dream workshops, watch documentaries, and read. What I learned is that dream deciphering is a personal job. Your dreams are meant for you. They're messages, information, and clues to things you need to know about, confront, deal with, or enjoy. (I opt for the—just enjoy!) It does make sense, though.

Another option is to drag your closest friends to the local watering hole to decode your outlandishly wacky dreams over your choice of libations and get their opinion! They know and care for you. They can often be the voice of reason, pointing out the symbology of what you have going on in your life. If you don't want to share, know that there are dream forums where you can submit your dream online and other users will tell you what they think it's about, again, colored by their experiences.

Does that make me an expert at my own dreams? Nope! Not yet! I am getting better, though. I know that my spirit guides and angels give me messages in my dreams I would say about 95 percent of the time. I hear the request a lot from the readers who read for me. "Pay attention to your dreams! We are giving you messages!" Yeah, yeah, yeah!

Ah, if it were only that easy to decode them. See, I like the KISS method. Seriously, I would love it if they would just say, "Go to the market and get some bread. The end." Do they? No! To me at times, my dream messages are the equivalent to dumping a one-thousand-piece puzzle in front of me. (I dream that much.) I saw all the pieces, but did I pay attention to them all? Probably not. But hey, there's always tonight's dream, right?

I was talking with someone and the subject of seeing a clock in your dream came up. I have never looked for or even been aware of a clock. I now have a new quest! They have seen a clock and saw the time. Then glanced back to recheck what was seen and discovered that it was many hours later.

Time does not exist in the dream realm. Ever take a snooze and feel like you just saw an entire movie in a dream to wake up and realize it was merely ten to fifteen minutes? Yup! So that's my new challenge to see a clock. Challenge accepted! Sweet dreams!

CHAPTER 33

MOUNTAIN: FLOAT AROUND VS. CLIMB – THAT IS THE QUESTION!

As I have mentioned, I run a practice group with very talented fellow woo-woo friends. When we get together, we exchange fun stories and share experiences, which raises our vibration before we get started.

During one of our more recent sessions, we teamed up and exchanged readings. My grandparents came through. OK, this was the perfect time to straight up ask if I should put any more effort into real estate in North Carolina (aka "climb the mountain") or just change lanes and be a channel for spirit (aka FLOAT).

My grandma came in first. She is one of my biggest cheerleaders as are my grandfather and great-aunt. They made my reader laugh as they brought their humor and personality through. Grandma applauded me for all that I have been doing. My great-aunt came through to pinch my cheeks and call me beautiful. Then, my grandpa came through with his humor and funny quips as well. I record my readings for future reference. Part of this reading went like this:

Did your grandfather pass away?

(YES)

He just came in and stood next to your grandmother.

(HI, GRANDPA!)

He is just there to let you know that he is there if you need him. Was he a big guy?

(SAME SIZE OR TALLER THAN GRANDMA.)

Is there anything you want to ask?

(IS GRANDPA DOING SOMETHING WITH THE RED BIRD? IS THAT HIM?)

He is showing me pecking at the window early in the morning to get your attention—he is laughing.

(YES!)

Does he have a sense of humor?

(YES! IS IT A WARNING? OR TO SAY HI?)

(pause) I think he would have told me if it was a warning but it's just to get your attention.

(HE'S DOING A GREAT JOB!)

He says, "*That's how we like to work on this side! That's going to be my signature bird from now on.*" He is coming in stronger now. He said, "*Don't worry about any guy or anything—he knows you have concerns but let her know I will be there!*"

(WELL SOMETIMES YOU'RE GOING TO HAVE TO LEAVE, GRANDPA! YOU DON'T NEED TO BE THERE FOR "ALL" THE STUFF!)

He is so funny! He's saying, "*Well the veil IS thin, you know!*" That is so funny! But as you know they can't see! He put his hand behind you and says, "*HE'S GOT YOU—wait, HE'S GOT YOU, GIRL,*" is what he is saying.

(CAN I ASK THEM A QUESTION?)

Sure!

(IS THE CURRENT WORK PATH I AM ON FLOATING AROUND THE MOUNTAIN OR CLIMBING IT?)

Climbing or floating? They are saying you're going through it—it's the image they gave but they all want to say *you got this*. They told me there're flowers on the other side if it makes you feel any better! Your grandfather is a stitch! Your grandmother is really sweet. But there is sunshine on the other side! It's great they are funny! They say you have the strength and perseverance to go through anything—you have the will and the strength! And your grandfather's saying, "*And you have us on the other side!*"

First, I had not given thought to them being around to see *everything* in a long time. It reminded me of the reader I went to that set boundaries with the spirits. Now the shoe was on the other foot, and I had abilities! Wow, a thin veil between worlds. They are everywhere!

Secondly, the answer they gave regarding my career was that I was going *through* the mountain. Honestly, that sounded right for how I felt.

You see, this question about my career had been heavy on my mind and soul. I felt like I knew the answer, but jumping out of it cold turkey meant complete blind faith that all my necessities would be taken care of. Unfortunately, the stubborn ego side of me that has done things a certain way, decided to take my innertube for safety with me and *then* try and climb the mountain.

Don't you love conundrums? Lately, spirit has been teaming up against my ego and mind. Trust me, spirit was winning, hands down.

I have been trying to get established in my thirty-plus-year career in the new area and having a really hard time. I'm not kidding, the more effort I put in, the higher my stress level got. My gut instinct was trying to talk to me, and I could not shake it. My hair was falling out—seriously, my tub drain was clogged. I was gritting my teeth and my jaw was tense. The stress level in my shoulders was painful and caused back issues. My left eye started twitching every time I headed to the office. STRESS-IS-NOT-FUN! Frankly, I hadn't even had this kind of stress since my divorce, so it *really* got my attention! I attributed the heavy stress to the learning curve and nuances of a brand-new area. I also questioned if the pushback I felt was because I wasn't done healing yet.

Being the trooper that I was, well, I ignored it one day too long. I knew what I was supposed to do. I was just fighting it. I knew the answer. I just didn't want to accept it. Why? It was uncharted territory for me. I have plans to do it my way! Do things *this* way, get *these* results and conquer *these* goals! Yeah, baby! Here I come!

There is a saying, *"If you want to make God laugh, tell him about your plans."* Let me tell you, he should have a hefty bruise from all the thigh-slapping laughter I have given him over the last few months. This subject was heavy on my heart. My plans had felt like an uphill battle for me.

Have I point-blank asked before? Yes. What did they tell me? Well, you could do your other job if you want, but *are you sure you want to*? (What happened to the yes or no answer?) Like the other signs I get, if I ignore one, they will keep at it to make sure I'm paying attention. That, they did.

I let the thought sit for two more days. Both days, the cards I pulled every morning for myself ruminated with my floating path. I asked other questions and every single sign indicated that I needed to float. As the magic eight-ball says, "All signs point to yes." I finally said, *"Fine, you win! Don't let me sink, please."*

I swear to you, it was like a twenty-five-pound weighted blanket was lifted off me. I prayed. I swear I could hear them dancing and cheering for me. (GOOOOOO, LISA!) I felt so much better! My decision to float felt right. That fast, I had resources suddenly appear and forwarded to me. My cards were all rainbows, butterflies, and unicorns. They weren't showing me the entire stream just a few feet in front of me. My pool float was now on.

Resigning my (fairly new) position and saying the right thing (for me) was important. I said a prayer and asked spirit to give me the right words to explain my intention to part ways and that being there was not the right path for me. I was honest and I spoke my truth. My boss believes in spirit guides herself. We had a really pleasant chat and she wished me well. I packed up my North Carolina office, surrendered my set of keys, and left.

I felt amazing relief. There was such a change in my energy level. Gone was the heaviness my soul was feeling. Things lined up one after the other. I know I made the right choice for my soul, and my journey. I am officially now one of those people who left the corporate world to follow my dreams even though I was keeping my license in the state.

My dreams and channeled messages were fast and furious. They revealed the next steps to happen in my future. The entire situation kind of reminds me of one of the last scenes from *The Wizard of Oz*—paraphrased, "You had the power all along, my dear; you had to find it out for yourself." Spirit cannot make decisions for you or live your life. You have free will. I had to come to the conclusion on my own.

So, right now, I am sitting on my float (new path)—floating. Do I know where I'm going? Nah, not exactly. But I am enjoying the view of the mountain that I'm floating around now. I don't know what's on the other side of the mountain, but my grandfather did say that not only would he be there for me, but he'd have flowers. As long as it's not a waterfall with rocks at the bottom on the other side of this "mountain" I'm supposed to go around, I think I can handle it.

The next batch of messages came in quickly!

To quote them, "*You have a cornucopia of events that will affect your life coming up.*" Ugh! Is it a waterfall? Is it good? Is it bad? Hey, I have more questions! Is there a seat belt on this float?

CHAPTER 34

NAME IT TO CLAIM IT

I have been told that I am a "master manifester" by a handful of people who have done readings for me. This sounds all cool and stuff, but I don't think I'm Jeannie from *I Dream of Jeannie*, whipping my hair around to make things happen. I don't have a magic lamp either—but I am looking for it! (If you have seen it, please send it to PO BOX ... oh, never mind!)

So manifesting is pretty much putting your intention out to the universe of what you want to have happen, acquire, or see. The key word is intention.

I can honestly look back and see that I got a lot of what I wanted. Unfortunately, some things came at a very steep price. See, before I truly knew what I was doing, or reading the book *The Secret*, I always said that if I wanted something bad enough, *"It's a done deal."* That was my motto.

I had no idea where all that resolve came from other than I fashioned myself as a strong, determined person. So, things I put my mind to seem to come to me. Mind you, not without work, because that's what we are supposed to do, right? Work for what we want.

Then when it comes, you often consider it the reward for your hard work and determination. Although sometimes, it seems more like a crazy coincidence!

I can look back and see many things in my life that I manifested. For example, as an extremely bored teenager in high school, one day, I created a list of things that I wanted in a boyfriend. I think it had, like, thirteen things. My rule was that until someone met everything on that list, I wasn't going to go out with them. What was important to me then were things like designer jeans, name-brand sneakers, and be athletic but not a super jock. Well, guess what I got? A boyfriend that fit all of that. I remember distinctly checking things off this list one day. *DING DING DING!* He got to pass Go and collect $200— I mean, he got Moi! (Trust me, my self-esteem was not as grand as I am making it out to be!) I think I conjured him up or was it a crazy coincidence? I was a teenager, what did I know?

The next big thing I remember strongly putting my intention toward was the sex of my kids. I only wanted boys (personal reasons too long to go into here). I knew darn well that I was going to be grateful, elated, and feel truly blessed with whatever was gifted to me from the heavens above. But trust me, in my silent prayers I exclaimed and literally begged that *I really really really only wanted boys.* Just for the record, hubby was not on board with this and wanted at least one daughter. Along came my amazing kids, both boys.

Did I have some superpower? Nope! Not that I was aware of, but somebody else thought I did though!

A few years later, I shared this "intention/desire/wish" with a former male friend from my old high school up north. I thought it was a fun, light-hearted discussion with a fellow parent until I got back a seething paragraph of "how *dare you* ask for a specific sex of a child" and a bunch of other mean comments. All because I wanted boys, and I got what I asked for.

I was in complete shock at what he wrote. Like, seriously? I paused and I gave thought to why he would be angry at me. I think my (unknown at the time) automatic writing skills kicked in. I remember being so calm about it. I wrote him back saying that I truly appreciated that he thought I had *that kind of power* to direct the heavens above to only give me what I wanted. I reminded him that I was grateful and would have been genuinely happy with whatever sex my children were. In my heart of hearts, my wish and desire were to only have boys. For that, I made no apologies. I had my reasons.

I guess whatever I said hit home. He apologized. He also explained that he had a son with a slight disability and was still angry over it.

Motoring along in life, I put my lofty intentions out to the heavens and declared things I wanted to do, places I wanted to go, or things I wanted to acquire. Mind you, I got quite a few squirrely looks from family and friends. What I was exclaiming exceeded what they accomplished. Therefore, they could not see little ole me exceeding their dreams. I never let that stop me. I wasn't going to listen to what their limited goals were and make them mine! Again, though, I truly didn't know how it was happening. Just blind faith that it was. If there was something I wanted, I confidently exclaimed, *it's a done deal*. I guess kind of like my own *abracadabra*! Then I waited. The majority of the time it showed up! I was like, how cool is this?

Did I know exactly what I was doing? Nope! After a while, the naysayers were not so vocal any longer. I even noted a few family members doing more of their own thing rather than listening to the limited beliefs of the conservative naysayers in the family and succeeding. I really just thought that everyone did it. How did I know they couldn't or didn't know how?

I want to stress that although I may present a very edited version of my life experiences thus far, it has most certainly has not been a cakewalk. There have been many lessons along my journey! Trust me!

A big lesson came at a work seminar I went to in California. I was having a rough time at home with massive stresses not caused by me, yet greatly affecting me. My usual happy-go-lucky disposition was fraught with endless mind chatter, sadness, and disbelief. That spiral of feelings seemed to bring forth more of the same. I would find the smallest glimmer of hope to hang on to, and even that went away. I was in what seemed like a whirlpool of never-ending quicksand. I could not pull myself up. Where had my magic mojo gone? I had zero hope in my eyes. Feeling beaten down and helpless, I welcomed the break of going bye-bye. Being more like a body filler than a participant during the seminar, something this speaker said truly resonated with me.

Suddenly, my soul was shown a glimmer down a potential path to get my "happy" back. I remember going back to my hotel and furiously writing out a plan. It was even broken down into how to get myself back up again with positive affirmations. Then, what I was going to do next and how it was going to happen. The fire was lit, and my passion was resurfacing with an infusion of hope I hadn't felt in a long while. I wanted my happy back. So, I claimed it.

You see, I realized I had given my power away. I realized I had surrendered my fate to circumstance to manifest for me. I was treading water waiting for the wind in my sails again to just appear. I realized it was *my job* to put wind in my own sails.

After that, things got going again. I was no longer the victim but the victor. I made myself happy and that attracted more happy moments. It was small steps at first, but I was grateful for them. That was a huge lesson learned. Be grateful and you will attract more to be grateful for! Also, don't give away your power!

Alas another big lesson came along. You know that saying, "Be careful what you wish for because you just might get it?" YUP-PERS! It happens just like that sometimes. Do I consistently get everything I put my mind to? Well, yes and no. There were, indeed, things I wanted badly, yet I now can see they were kept out of my reach for a reason. Did I know it or why? Nope. To me it just meant try harder. (I may or may not admit I am stubborn at times. Just saying.)

I will admit that I had a few temper tantrums about certain subjects that I wanted really, really badly. Well, I did finally get something that I was wishing upon the stars for. Repeatedly. Day in and day out. I think the angels were just fed up with me and said, *"Fine! Let her have it!"*

Something finally showed up that kind of looked like what I wanted, and I claimed it! Man, I grabbed on and held tight!

Yep! I finally got it alright! Having it? Sheesh, it was like trying to push a car with square wheels through the Sahara Desert. I could not understand why it was so-dang-hard when other things were so easy! Now? I can look back and see that although I manifested it to happen, it was not meant for me. Thus, the constant resistance to me getting it, which was why it was not so easy!

Did finally getting what I whined about turn out great? Not at all! Don't even get me started on this one! Oh, I got what I wanted all right, along with many years of lessons because of it. So, the lesson learned was that if it is not easy, double-check. There may indeed be a reason that it is not for you.

Many lessons and blessings later, along with my faith, I was more cautious of exactly what I was trying to manifest! Then the movie *The Secret* came out and the buzzword "manifesting" became more mainstream. Did I realize spirit was helping me? No. I just prayed a lot and found things to keep my energy up. Happy brings forth more things to be happy about. My job? Stay happy!

Another lesson I learned about all this was "from the outside in." I took this one as a warning shot of sorts. You see, a friend of mine mentioned she wanted to quit smoking. She didn't smoke much but knew she wanted to eliminate the habit once and for all. Of course, as all our well-intended New Year's resolutions are, she couldn't quite kick it on her own. Then, suddenly, she got really, really, sick. Like, she couldn't breathe without labored effort. It really took her a few months to rid herself of the lingering cough. BUT! Guess what? She doesn't smoke anymore. Note taken!

As my connection with the spirit world has evolved, I sincerely know that everything happens for a reason. Thinking about how this went down, I realized how involved angels are in helping us get or prevent what we are trying to manifest. Indeed, my friend's angels helped her when she couldn't do it on her own. At the time, neither one of us really understood what went down until we were eating lunch one day and the subject of her lingering cough came up. I reminded her that the side effect was that she got what she wanted. She had stopped smoking. Trust us, that put us both in check about quite a few things! We *both* received a lesson.

Spirit wants you to think about and consider what you are manifesting and why. They will make sure to put resistance if it is not the right thing, time, or circumstance. It's kind of like them saying *are you sure?* Be aware that bad energy or intention attract more of the same. You may imply to those around you that you are just being nice, but spirit knows your true intent. You can't have bad thoughts and expect great results. It is your sign to pay attention to and, hopefully, figure it out. Sometimes it is in the form of the proverbial green light or a ton of resistance, so you back up. Either way, you can look back at your life and see in the rearview mirror what was or was not supposed to happen and most times the reason why.

So, of late, spirit is encouraging me to really think about what the big picture is supposed to look like for me going forward. I have been given a great big crayon and a blank piece of paper to color any way I want. They want me to think about what I want to manifest going forward. Jeez, with all the lessons I have learned, I am a bit more cautious about what that looks like. Jokingly, they call this part of me "analysis paralysis." I used to just blindly do things but now I am careful about what I want to manifest.

I recently had a run of things I manifested that spirit put in front of me. I did it so blindly that I believe that in itself was also part of a lesson to just do it. Seriously, for about a week, I thought it and whatever it was, it just showed up! It was like they were showing me how easy it could be again.

Ultimately, I know that it was another lesson for me to not make manifesting harder than it needed to be. After all, there are also lessons in standing still and doing nothing! Having had some seriously hard lessons, well, who wouldn't tread lightly when creating the path forward?

I know I am protected and divinely guided. If it is meant for you on your path for one reason or another, it's going to appear. You will see a sign. You must be grateful. Find gratefulness in the smallest things until you find more. Like attracts like. Keep raising your vibration.

So, wish upon a star, make that vision board, say your prayers with conviction, speak to your angels, guardians, guides and loved ones. Let them know what you are grateful for and what you desire. A lesson or a blessing will result, either way, you learn, and win. Keep the faith!

CHAPTER 35

DOUBLE-TALK. WHAT DID YOU MEAN?

O nce upon a time, I had a friend who was pretty darn skilled in the art of "double-talk." When I spoke with them, I was led in one direction by their words. They never implied it was any different. Suddenly when it served their purpose, they would say they intended it to be another way. Honestly, I could not dispute it. It could indeed, be how they said it.

Once I caught onto this, frankly, it fascinated me. It almost became a game to figure out all the way's this friend could conjure up the intended meaning. For example, they would describe someone as being "hot." I might take this to mean they are very attractive, and my friend would never correct or clarify my interpretation. Only later when I confronted them would they imply they meant different than what I assumed.

As curious as I was as to what was being said, I was duly amazed at how skilled they were at doing it. I would watch their interactions with others, knowing their game, and see firsthand what they were doing. Personally, I came from the school of making sure that you say what you mean and mean what you say. I have steadily tried to be very clear in my conversations to avoid this kind of confusion. Were they? Nope.

Holy cow this was a skillful art! I studied this friend with complete fascination. I questioned their need to speak a statement so vague that no matter what the circumstances they were at liberty to say you were wrong. They never accepted responsibility. There was a smugness when they would point the finger at you to avoid accountability by saying it was how *you* took it. Of course, I realized I could never take what this person said at face value any longer. They proved themselves masterful in manipulating the circumstances with their intended vagueness. It was a lesson though for me. Take what this person said with a grain of salt. I bet you have a friend or two like this!

Fast forward to now. I have wanted so desperately to hang my hat on what I am told through my intuition, channeling, and messages of upcoming events at face value. More often than not, my messages are exactly black and white and frankly very clear. I ask for them to be that way so there is no question in my mind!

Other messages, not-so-much. Spirit gives me a message that, to me, are double-talk. Of course, again, it's my interpretation of what spirit is telling me through the lens of my experiences at that exact moment. I want the puzzle piece of information/guidance they give me to be easily identifiable, marked accordingly, and explicitly clear so I can go to the next one. That's when I get the proverbial finger waved in my face going, AH, AH, AH! ... ARE YOU SURE?

UGH! Well not *anymore*! (Picture me with an exasperated expression.)

So why would spirit be so forward, blunt, and exact on so many things but then give you a "double-talk" piece? I don't think there is a textbook answer to this. Personally, I haven't figured out the official wording to explain it just yet. I admit I have used some *ahem* "choice words" in my frustration at times.

The best way I can somewhat summarize why spirit may do it this way is to indeed make sure I am given the notification as requested yet they won't allow me to fully comprehend for a reason not disclosed to me. Why? So, I learn to pause, see how things turn out and not race to a finish line. Not only does spirit want me to pay attention to this nebulous piece they put in front of me, it's also to make sure I become aware that this is an important piece that I need to know even though it is not fully seen yet!

Here's an example: Through a series of events, you believe you are going down the most appropriate street. Because you are fast thinking you know you got this! You see a street and immediately think that's the one! Then you glance around and realize you are at the intersection of seven freakin' roads that all look the same. Which one is it? AHA! That's where you must wait for the next clue, step or nudge. But, oh, if you become impulsive and not pause (sing my game show speaker voice here as spirit),

BOB! TELL HER WHAT SHE WINS!

(Bob) Lisa, CONGRATULATIONS! You get a life lesson!

If you guess right? You get to pass Go and collect $200 (that was for all my Monopoly fans). You see, the key word in this was "appropriate." Well, appropriate how and for whom? Was it the easiest road with nothing in your way? Or was the better road one with potholes and a tree lying across it? How do you interpret what is or is not appropriate?

Being honest, I struggle with this a lot. I know the lesson in all of this is to wait for further signs. Yes, spirit wants me not to be so impulsive. Yet the other side of the coin is waiting too long and missing opportunities. I have seen so many others miss them I tend to be probably more impulsive than I need to be.

So, spirit "double-talks," giving me a puzzle piece that could be implied and interpreted too many ways to count. I am onto them and know they are doing this. Do I still take that one puzzle piece and try fitting it into every conceivable scenario? YES-I-DO. Do they give me the answer because I tried really, really hard? NO-THEY-DON'T. Grrr!

Unlike my friend who proved to me I cannot trust anything they say because of their exquisite skills of double-talk, I absolutely trust my guides. Admittedly at times, reluctantly. I recognize that spirit does not do it to me all the time. It's probably why I am aware of it when it happens. So, I wait for the next clue or direction to define what it really means. It is also to remind me that because I like to work fast, I need to enjoy the journey and smell the roses a bit more than I do.

Do I like it? No. It scares the crap out of me sometimes. I have learned so many lessons because I rushed and tried to do it my way. There is a reason for the double-talk. *They don't want me to know yet.* The harder I look for the exact meaning, the more potential explanations they show me. My vision gets increasingly blurrier and my head spins.

The good news is that I at least recognize the double-talk now. When I am aware of it, it's an internal struggle not to use all my energy looking for the exact explanation of what I am told. You know, to find an exact fit of the circumstances at the moment. On occasion, I may or may not give it the "ole college try" and work myself into analysis paralysis. Yes, that is when I have not only seen the seven different ways the message could be taken but create five more of my very own!

I know what spirit does is out of love. They have shown and proved to me more times than I care to admit, that not only do they know the words and secret intents of those around us that we cannot, but how to protect me.

There are many moving parts in all of our lives, not all apparent. Some will affect us now and some that will in the future.

The good news is, if you practice being aware of the double-talk message, you know to be aware of more clues to come forth. It's only looking back that you can go *holy crap, so that's what those words meant*. More often than not, it wasn't even close to the probability you created. (Spirit is sneaky like that.)

Just know that they are aligning the other puzzle pieces of your life for experiences and events to help move you where you need for the next chapter. Until then, pause when you don't know what something means. Ask for clues and hints to show you the most appropriate path and keep asking to see the front of the puzzle box!

CHAPTER 36

NOW YOU SEE ME, NOW YOU DON'T

Guess what? The state parks are finally opened in my town after being closed because of COVID! WOO-HOO! My favorite one has opened its gates. You would have thought I won the lottery by how excited I was to discover this. Being allowed back in the parks after isolating during the world plague was like Christmas morning to me. I was even armed with a new bag of peanuts to feed the squirrels. I have not been able to visit, and they must be starving without me! The gates officially opened, and I went in.

Requiring my overdue dose of trees and forest, I decided to set out and get my exercise in with a hike and then my reward would be to feed the squirrels. They are quite entertaining!

I ventured onto a new path almost breaking out into song. The weather was cool, and the trees had their new coat of fresh spring leaves. I take music along to listen to, but I find a lot of times that silence on the walk is just as good. It lets your mind sort itself out which, for me, lets me sleep better!

If you had seen me in passing you would have thought the local forestry service hired me to be a park greeter. Yesterday, I talked to everyone who was out on a hike, it seemed. I was doing my "job" being vocal and yet social distancing. To some it must have seemed like I was running for local office.

So, I arrived at my distance-destination before I was going to turn back and saw a big hill to go down should I go further. Of course, what goes down must come back up. Um ... "Not today," said my legs.

I decided to stop and simply appreciate the beauty of the woods, shade, and trees. Trust me when I say I'm easily entertained at times! It was *so quiet*. So, I decided a "council meeting" was in order. My council meetings are me praying out loud and the trees listening. I must say, I have a very captivating audience! (Wink! wink!)

I enjoy the woods when I need to talk or make big decisions. The trees comfort me as much as the ocean does. Spirit is around me, listening to me ramble. BLAH BLAH BLAH. I wonder if the trees clap and shake their leaves when I leave? Get it? When I "leave"? Anyway, when I am there, I just talk out loud. I know that angels are listening, whether I can see them or not.

I would like to think that the trees missed me since my "council meetings" have been on hold while the parks were closed for so long. So, being in a new area of the park, I looked around. I hadn't seen anyone for quite a few minutes, actually! I heard nothing. It was unbelievably quiet and peaceful! I looked to the left and then to the right, then back left again. NOT-A-SOUL was around. Well except for the spirits of course. Not a rustle of leaves. Just me. I just wanted to talk out loud in my prayerlike jabber I do. The coast was clear.

HERE YE, HERE YE! THE COUNCIL MEETING IS NOW IN SESSION!

Considering I had been warned of some not-so-fun events coming up, I just wanted to say a few words asking for additional divine protection around not only my immediate family but also for my stepchildren from my last marriage. I then decided to speak to my dear friend in spirit from high school (who also is my ex-sister-in-law) who passed away, Dorothy.

Dorothy has come through to me over different events in the past few years, gifting me messages from her and her mom (whom I never met while she was alive). When she has something to say, she will make sure I see her name repeatedly, so I pause and listen. Anyway, I asked for Dorothy and her mom to please place protection around her niece and nephew, who were my stepchildren, regarding concerns I had. Here is where it got remarkably interesting!

I want to stress that this was not a long, drawn-out prayer by any stretch of the imagination. I think myself a fast talker at times. No sooner had I said to Dorothy, "Please place protection around your niece and nephew," than suddenly a girl stood to my left. I heard nothing of her approach at all! To me, she looked like a deer in headlights, and I must have appeared the same to her. My heart pounded fiercely but simultaneously I felt at such peace!

She asked me if I was OK.

I said, "Yes, I am just praying." (I felt very emotional for a moment as well!)

She said, "Praying is good" and put her hands together. She added, "I will pray with you if you want."

It seemed awkward for a stranger to want to pray with me in the woods, so I assured her that I was fine and asked her what her name was.

DOROTHY.

I instantly had a feeling this was *so not a coincidence*. I told her I was just praying to my friend, Dorothy, at that exact moment! Goose bumps covered my body.

She paused and smiled at me. We chatted for a few minutes as a few people and their dogs passed by. She was so friendly. I felt comfort talking with her. Finally, we parted ways, and I gave her a two-minute head start while I finished up the last part of my prayers. I looked to see how far ahead she was ... And she was gone.

G-O-N-E.

Like as fast as she appeared she was *POOF*, gone!

I want to stress that she had on a white tank top. White stands out in the brown and green woods. She also had a lime green water bottle on her waistband. Not only did I not hear anything, but I didn't see anything. I even followed the same path she was on! She disappeared as fast as she appeared.

There are no "coincidences" in life. Things that are meant to be will show up when they are meant to, sometimes to draw your attention to a subject repeatedly, and sometimes when you need an angelic presence.

I truly feel that Dorothy made an earthly appearance to give me comfort and acknowledge my prayers during my "council meeting." It did not stop me from being in jaw-dropping awe of what just had transpired. You can't make this shit up!

Of course, I still am scratching my head in wonderment. Despite having had these cool experiences, my human side still questions things. I even called a few friends and told them what happened while in the parking lot. They had goose bumps in confirmation. I did speak out and say *thank you* to her after the fact.

I never sat down to feed the squirrels. The poor things are probably still starving! I was in such a daze that I just headed home. Rest assured; I am going back. There will, indeed, be more things to discuss now that "council" is back in session! Wonder who will show up at my next council meeting?

Dear reader, I encourage you to spend time in nature where and however you can. It is good to ground your energy and just be silent.

You never know what you might learn!

CHAPTER 37

DATING ADVICE FROM SPIRIT

GROUNDED! After my divorce, I gave myself a time-out. No dating. No canoodling with the opposite sex. I didn't impose a time limit. Whatever time it took was how long I needed. I needed to heal, had to figure out how to put down the baggage. Separate out what was mine, and what belonged to others. I needed to breathe. I had to figure out who the hell I was, what I liked and what I didn't like. I had to take ownership of my part of my patterns and why. I had to dig deep and know what lessons I had (*finally*) learned so I don't *ever* do them again!

It was time to recenter. Learn about taking care of me first and what it looked like moving forward. I promise that was the short version. In general, though, this is what spirit calls doing your "shadow work." So, I did what I do best—retreat.

Oh, my battered heart! The only way I knew to let it heal was to build a fortress around it. Man, I got a five-gallon bucket of Gorilla Glue, mixed it with quick-dry cement, bought a mountain of cinder blocks, found an island that had a mote with alligators in it and promptly walled my heart off from the world. No more! It was a tower that rivaled Rapunzel's! No windows or doors anywhere! At the time ... it was for good.

Like anything traumatic, the scars were fresh and very deep. When, and IF, I healed remained to be seen. Love was officially forgotten. I told my heart that I was sorry. I would occasionally peek in to see how the healing was going. It was truly a very-slow-process. I even became allergic to romantic movies, steamy novels, and couples showing deep compassionate love toward one another. It was like poking a deep bruise. I avoided those scenarios at all costs! Love?

Blah blah blah ... *WHAT-EV-ER*! ... NEXT!

Time went on and I started getting some indication that the fortress was starting to crack. A few years had gone by already! Had it been that long? I was very much aware of certain aspects of myself that were starting to resurface. What? Someone was actually good-looking? No way, Jose! I even noticed that my allergic reaction to movies about love or songs on the radio was not there. It wasn't a good feeling, but it also was no longer a bad feeling. I no longer felt disdain, anger, or disgust. Hark! Was there progress? It was really pretty cool to see some small cracks in my fortress. I didn't work to wedge them open, but I was just noticing them.

During one of my channeling sessions, spirit showed me a red heart in a tower. The heart was starting to push out of the confines of the walls that held it captive and face the light again. That vision spoke volumes to me! My heart was chipping away at the walls from the inside and emerging stronger, fuller, bigger than before, albeit with a new set of rules!

Spirit told me I had to meet my newly healed heart for the first time and get acquainted. It wasn't the same as before. Then, my heart and I had a serious talk! I went over the list of things that were no longer allowed. Non-negotiables! I reviewed the things I didn't ever want again and turned them into the opposite, looking at what I did want. My heart was very clear that it would no longer entertain anything that wasn't the right fit. So, I had to make sure I had the new rules down pat and what my boundaries are. The biggest one for me: *what it looks like to take care of MY HEART first.*

So, my heart and I now have an agreement. The tattoo that read "BOYS ARE YUCKY" has been covered up. (And yes, "yucky" is a technical term.)

I have to tell you there has been zero discussion about this at all with anyone. I was just going to let it all sit for a while. No rush! Just make sure I feel good about everything when I check back in a few weeks. But then, I had a friend pass along random messages to me from spirit on dating. It seems like my heart is sending out an SOS to my spirit guides for some help! I'm not sure if I want to call my heart a show-off or a traitor!

I LOVE MY SPIRIT GUIDES! Oh, my Lord, are they so damn funny! Of late, the way they have been giving messages to me through my counterparts is in cartoons. You heard that right! I think that is so clever! It has been enjoyable being the sitter and, for them, the reader! (Honestly, this was probably the only way I would listen and not shut the messages out.) Now, mind you, I have not asked about this topic at all to anyone! I'm just accepting that my newly healed heart was enjoying being in the sun for the moment. So, trust me when I tell you, this has been out of left field to get these messages! I tell others that spirit gives you what you need—not necessarily what you want! This is a clear example. I see Mufasa from *The Lion King* in my head, his deep, booming voice saying, "IT IS TIME." I guess my heart needs to get back in shape. Suddenly, my message became about dating.

You see, spirit has jumped in to explain the (new) law of the land for me. Yep, spirit is now giving me "dating advice." Oh, if you could hear the thigh-slapping laughter from how they phrased things for me! *HA-LAR-IOUS!* My friend who gave me this reading said, "*OMG! They are hard on you! This is so funny!*"

They used the animated films *The Princess and The Frog* and *The Boss Baby* to explain it to me. So, here we go! Grab some popcorn for this one! Most of this is literally verbatim!

Messages from spirit on me dating:

#1 – We are "shaking you out of your tree." You are not allowed to hide anymore.

#2 – You are going to be presented with many FROGS—ONE WILL BE THE PRINCE. Get to kissin'! (She saw me kissing a lot of frogs!)

#3 – These frogs we are sending are a test. These are only a test. (I think they are concerned I might mess it up!) We need to see if you know when to send them back to the pond. We need you to practice speaking up about your needs and wants. We want to see if you get it right!

"Ribbit"

#4 – Practice being dainty. Let things happen! Don't try and control, cut and run. You don't/won't have to do that anymore.

#5 – Give people a chance! Do not base what you see on one date to be the entire picture. Capeesh?

#6 – (And I quote) "Do not come home from a date and ask us if he is the one. We won't tell you!" (That's exactly what I would do!) I think there were a solid three to four minutes of roaring laughter out of me for that statement. They so know me! Hey! I got connections! Of *course*, I'm going to ask! Wouldn't you?

#7 – Practice being led. Your input on how that looks is not part of this. If the man in your life wants to take you on a picnic lunch— allow them to plan it all and don't ruin it! (Who … MOI?)

#8 – We take *great joy* in bringing someone to you. You will also know by a distinct flower they give to you. (Spirit told me of this flower years ago so I know!)

#9 – Draw the 'boss' side of you back. This will be an equal counterpart. You don't need to be the boss all the time anymore. This is not a boss baby in a diaper. This is a boss-MAN!

#10 – Here's a clue, because we know you are going to ask—*it will NOT be someone from your past*. No riffraff!

#11 – They are giving you a lot of credit for being willing to try again and not shut down.

#12 – Learn to receive—there is a "silver platter" being presented to you. The more you allow, the more you will receive.

#13 – We angels are orchestrating this. We are selecting this person for you. *You are not.* This is heavenly made for you.

#14 – This person has done the work—worked through *their* shadow side. Do not judge them on their shadows! He is not "heaven" but "heaven-sent," so he has a bad-boy edge to him (silently I'm jumping up and down, shh!) But it's not who you usually go for. (AHA! Another piece to the puzzle!)

#15 – See the person first, then go check your list. (Yes, I have a list) Give them a chance. See them through your third eye (intuition). Don't compare them to your list out of the gate.

#16 – We know you won't tolerate anything "less-than."

#17 – TRUST THE PROCESS.

#18 – You will know the frog that is the prince because (and I quote!) Poof! You will *know*! (She really said, "Poof!")

I love them for doing this for me! I sound insanely difficult, don't I? I'm not! They spoke of every conceivable way I have *ever* asked for confirmation to make sure that no matter what, I can't dispute anything. It's truly an act of GOD for me to even try again. I had no idea that this would be the message. Jeez, I'm still giggling over all of this!

What a blessing to have spirit look out for me in all of this and vocalize it! My friend from the woo-woo practice group was the microphone. She was the perfect person. She has a fantastic personality, doesn't know this side of me at all, and her delivery made the words enjoyable to hear as much as the message given. It was raw and blunt, which is how I needed to hear it but funny as all get out!

We both enjoyed the comedic way it was delivered through her. The laughter did both of our souls good!

Honestly, I appreciate that there will be some "practice frogs." After a long road of recovery, no doubt I will stumble taking my first few steps again. I need to find my footing, watch my steps, and practice applying the "new" rules for my heart to stay healthy. That will involve taking care of ME before anyone else.

So, if you see a trail of frogs in my wake, just know that I didn't step on them. I just shooed them back toward the pond. May they be someone else's Prince Charming.

Hey, I have to run and put some lipstick on. Pucker up, frogs! Here I come! OK, well maybe tomorrow!

CHAPTER 38

LEARNING TO STAND IN YOUR POWER

You know the times when words and phrases have been repeated so much you start to detest what they are? This was one for me: **Stand in your power**. OK, WHAT power? I don't have a cape or wear a big "S" on my chest!

A few years ago, I visited a friend of mine. As we compared stories, just talking about life, she said something about my "power." I had no clue what she was talking about.

In trying to describe it to me, she asked me why I felt like it was better for me to be seen without standing out. She reminded me that once upon a time, I used to stand out, but now I just shrink back. She thought me a force to be reckoned with! Sadly, my answer rolled off my tongue with such conviction that I truly didn't know where it came from.

"Because when I stand in my power and line up, it's going to hurt some people." I was baffled by my own statement. Who the hell said that? She digested what I said and after a moment, she concurred that I was indeed, pretty powerful.

Having said that, I want to clarify what that means to MOI. It's the moment when I am "on." This is more than a life-gasm moment. It's like, the stars are super bright out. The weather is perfect. The birds all sing when I walk by, and you have "that" feeling. Some people might call it an "invincible feeling." Well, that's what it is like to me when I am in my power. I'm strong and determined. It's different for everyone, though. What might be power to me could be insignificant to you. That's OK!

Anyway, I left my friend with self-assigned homework to dig around in my bag of tricks to find out where this said power was that I once had. Furthermore, why it left! I also had to come to terms with what I exclaimed about not wanting to hurt some people. Like, what did that entail?

All I knew was that for a window of time I felt powerLESS. The light that used to shine so strong and bright from happiness, desire, dreams and conviction was now, well, I didn't know where it went. I didn't even know how long it had been gone. It wasn't something that disappeared instantly. It was a slow disintegration that I did not realize was happening.

Looking back, I just kept adjusting myself to whatever was going on as the new normal, instead of being in my own power and standing taller.

I had to ask myself, when was the last time I felt powerful? I dug up a moment and recalled how I felt. Now, I had a benchmark to work from. *That* was my power my friend was talking about. So… OK, I was onto something. I wasn't sure exactly what it all entailed but I knew that something was there.

It's intriguing how spirit works moments into your life, so you take notice. One evening, as I was headed home from work, a feeling suddenly came over me that all the drivers were getting irritated with me, and I was "bothering" them. It wasn't even in rush hour traffic, let alone on a busy road. I sped up to get into the turn lane to turn into my neighborhood quickly because I (wait for it!) didn't want the person behind me to be mad at me.

OOOOH, OOOOH! Let me say it for you and state how insanely ridiculous that thought was! Holy cow! Sadly, that was where I had gotten to. So, excuse the French here, but WHAT-THE-HELL? Seriously? Did I acknowledge that my driving on the road was somehow irritating people and that I should feel bad about it? Did I actually feel bad that I inconvenienced them because I was on the road at the same time?

Sadly, yes, I did. I'm not proud of it, trust me.

Let me tell you, *that* experience right there was the straw that broke the camel's back. In that instant, it was like my angels took over driving, and made me pull off the side street and stop the car. I could hear them say to me, "*OK, that's it! We are talking right now!*" I felt outside my body watching me scold myself. Unreal!

I was so mad at myself! That night there was a massive lesson spirit made for me. My angels made sure I understood. I was so *not* in my power that I was concerned that a stranger might be mad at me. How ridiculous is that? (Go ahead, you can say it!)

At that moment, on the side of the road and only two streets away from my home, a whirlwind of emotions came upon me. The tears started. I was mad and ashamed that I had let myself get to that point! A plethora of feelings overwhelmed me. This was not me at all. Spirit made sure I got the message loud and clear. How did I get to this point? Alas, it was a starting point to see how truly powerless I had allowed myself to become. Knowing this helped me to stop the bleeding and get back to power again. Note taken!

Was I fixed by that one instance? Oh, hell no! I felt aware but certainly not fixed. No, siree! I had to face that I had some very big underlying issues that needed to be addressed. I thought about taking a general survey of those around me, but I decided to work on this little project myself.

Another "duh" moment came for me from a friend. Don't you love friends who bring lessons? Not! I admit, we were slightly competitive about certain things, but not things you would normally think. It was goofy stuff! One Saturday, we were comparing what we each accomplished for the day. I was plum proud that I push-mowed my grass. (I *love* cutting the grass!) My friend bragged that they used a ride-on lawn mower. For some reason, I had it instilled into my head that because I push-mowed, I was a harder worker. My friend, realizing I was looking for an extra star for my efforts, looked at me and said, "Just because you chose to work harder doesn't make your accomplishment any better. I just chose to work smarter by using a ride-on lawn mower."

If you could have heard the loud glass-crash effect in my head. *MIND BLOWN*, WOW! That one stung! It made me realize how much I hung my hat on the fact that my power and efforts were only valued if I worked harder than everyone else. (Funny how no one had ever pointed that out to me before.) I learned many lessons from this friend over the years. This was one of many. The bigger question was, why did I not see this in myself?

One of the biggest realizations that I was not in my power, and still struggle with to this day, deals with airlines. You know that long and boring lecture we all ignore when we fly? (Except for the funny ones! Those I listen to with full interest!) You've heard it: "In case of loss of cabin pressure, place the oxygen mask over your own face before helping someone else." I kind of still have a problem with this! Why? Because I want to help everyone! I absolutely would be the person who helped the person next to me first.

I really don't understand why this is not right. Someone pointed out to me that therein lies the issue at hand. Your power is to take care of you first. THAT-IS-YOUR-JOB. The other person needs to take care of themselves. That is *their* job! (Children and elderly do not apply here.) I was still not acknowledging my power by putting the needs of others before me. I was not taking care of MOI first.

So now that I had three very clear examples pointed out to me (well, OK, there were WAY more, but I am only going to admit to three), I addressed my earlier comment about possibly hurting people if I stand in my power. You see, when you're in your power and don't allow people to walk all over you and create boundaries, some people get mad. They claim you hurt them because you didn't allow them to walk all over you. You hurt them when you say no or when you set boundaries. Just because they are mad, doesn't make them right! If it is not to their benefit, they get mad and butthurt. They expect your forgiveness every time they did something wrong. If not, you hurt them. I could point out more. Unfortunately, this was a glaring example of what not being in my power looked like. I had to come to terms with the fact that I was going to lose "friends" because I wouldn't tolerate that behavior any longer, because they were "hurt." No one was standing up for me. That was my job.

Don't you love learning curves? When the student is ready, the teacher will appear! These lovely examples were brought to my attention for me to finally see very clearly. My angels made it feel like a time-out review and I did not like what I saw. I finally got it, though. Through the examples of what not being in my power looked like, I was now able to define what standing in my power looked like. It is drawing a line in the sand to say *NO*. It's defending what you believe in and what you expect. It's not backing down. Standing in your power doesn't have to be loud. I don't have to shout or get mad. I just need to speak the hell up and be OK if someone else doesn't agree with me. I am in charge of me. This is my power. Handle it! Guess what? People get over it and move on to someone else that hasn't realized how to stand in their power.

That was my lesson in all of this. It's OK if someone else feels slighted because you took care of what is important to you. Most of all, know who you are but also who you aren't. Know inside what you're capable of. It's the foundation and essence of you at the very core. Finally, you owe no one an explanation. Although, at times, we all feel compelled to explain. (Hush! I'm workin' on it!)

In closing, I would like to announce that my thesis: *Standing In Your Power* is pretty much done. Unless of course, my angels decide to create a pop quiz.

Oh, it's been a long road to get here, all right. I still fight the urge to work harder and not smarter on occasion. (Hey, old habits are hard to shake!) Being aware helps. I have pulled my big girl britches up under my chin! Let's hope the elastic holds.

CHAPTER 39

ALLERGIC TO PATIENCE

I was looking for some all-encompassing "Confucius" joke or meme to reflect all the things I have to say about being "patient." It is like this four-letter word sometimes in my life! I also want to stress that I am great at dishing out info about it but rather horrible at taking the advice.

I've tested positive. I am allergic to patience. Mostly. Now, I do have patience about a lot of things, but I am a planner. I have the skill set and desire of wanting to work ahead. That's what this is about: Wanting to work ahead.

I know and tell people all the time; "Let the universe line things up for you." (Aka be patient) But when it comes to me? Nope, nope, and oh, yeah, nope!

Even while thinking about how I wanted to structure this commentary on the subject, a Joel Osteen radio show had the topic of learning patience. (You can't make this stuff up!) He pointed out that when you are feeling impatience, do you notice that you seem to find more things that cause you to have a lack of patience? (YES!) On top of hearing that, coincidentally, a clip of the movie *Evan Almighty* just showed up on my social media. It's the scene where God shows up to sit with Evan's impatient wife and says, "*Let me ask you something. If someone prays for patience, you think God gives them patience? Or does he give them the opportunity to be patient?*"

You would think that being connected to my angels and spirit guides that I might have the inside scoop on timing of events so I can plan. Sometimes? Yes! Right now? Not happening! The human side of me is having a battle with this currently. I want to take care of these unknown things and events *right now* and spirit to me is saying, "In a minute. I'm watching this snail travel across Europe!"

What the hell!

Now, in some ways, being void of patience is a form of anxiousness. (Oh, I can see my angels clapping their hands for me as this realization just came to me as I was typing!) Me wanting to get things taken care of ahead of time, under my terms, is so that *I'm* in control and know the outcome. (Jeez, can't we all just play by my rules?) So, say it with me, "When you are anxious about something, you are not present in the moment" Whatever! Blah blah blah.

I just live with the premise that if you work ahead, you have more free time! Like getting the grass cut and the laundry done before the weekend allows you to have more free time to do fun stuff, right? So, when I am aware that things are coming up and I want to address them and be prepared, *why can't I?* When I do practice patience, at times, I feel like a procrastinator.

Inevitably when it is time for you to know, it's mostly when you will have *no time or patience*. Coincidence? I think not. Perfect timing to teach you a lesson? Of *course*! Make you look at things differently? Sigh, yes. Make you address your priorities differently? Show you a possible *better* or *easier* path than the one you were going to race down? Yes. Spirit knows what is best for you even if we don't agree with it. *(Your Honor? I object!)*

Does knowing and dishing out all this "great advice" make me *take* it better? Hell no! I have been told that some pretty big things are coming up for me and I would like to know about them right now. Can I see a show of hands of those who are in agreement with me?

There was a quote from Chelsea Clinton that said, "*Impatient people get things done.*" Yes. We. Do. I was that person who worked ahead to get my term papers done and then enjoyed smug satisfaction when my counterparts were stressing to get theirs done at the last minute.

But again, let's go back. The more you want to get things done on your terms is the time spirit will intentionally make you wait. Why? In my case it is to remind me that I am not in charge!

We have become such an impatient society that is all about instant gratification. We no longer have the patience to wait. I think when we look back at what is going on with this COVID experience, we will see what a gift it was to slow down and be more patient and grateful for the time and hopefully stop being in such a rush.

In learning this, I see mini lessons along the way when I am in a hurry. Like, suddenly being stuck in traffic and hitting every single light. Or, when you have a deadline to meet, you stumble across unforeseen obstacles. While being a workaholic for a few years, I noticed I worked best in a state of chaotic frenzy. No patience, just go-go-go! My friends and I run *circles* around some of our other friends! Tornados did not have anything on us when we were in a mood to get things done.

Alas ... my pixie dust is not there. Why? Because spirit and my angels are trying to teach me about the virtuous notion of patience by taking it to the next level. I just want to work ahead and lay out the plan for the next things to come.

Are they are giving me hints? Sure, they are! Things like "*It will happen when it happens.*" (To me this statement is the equivalent of your parents saying *because I said so*.) Then there are the "two more weeks," "three more months" stuff. So, I wait. Now spirit tells me: "*Because you keep asking, we don't think you have quite learned the lesson yet. We now sentence you to an additional three weeks to nine months. We will see.*"

In trying to describe how I feel about this to my friends, it is like standing there turning around in circles looking for what might come to pass and never seeing it. Trust me, my human side has had a few choice words to say about whatever this thing is that never seems to show up. I now understand that when we think we are doing good by working ahead, we might not be getting all the pieces we need to do it *correctly*. Why can't spirit encourage patience when it comes to homework, dishes, or laundry?

I just want to get a head start ... SHOW ME THE PIECES TO THE PUZZLE AND HOW THEY ARE GOING TO FIT. LET ME SEE THE FRONT OF THE PUZZLE BOX. I am willing to do the work! Can't I get a hint?

Through my channeling, spirit has been telling me of things to come. My woo-woo friends confirm that there is most definitely something on the horizon and *they* can't even see it. I admit, I decided to cheat (in case an angel was slacking) and pull cards to see if I could get a smidgen of a hint. When I point-blank asked? The card that came out said, "*It's a secret.*" I busted out laughing at that one.

Time on the spirit side is fluid. There are no clocks in the angelic realm. When it's meant to be, it will be. That's how time is. The end.

In pulling out some messages I had received over a year ago, I noticed that this "doozy" of a time that is headed for me has been mentioned to me for about a year! Does that count for patience? I have warned all my friends monthly, thinking *this is it* and nothing has happened (well, to the extent I think it was supposed to). So, like the little boy who cried wolf, when things actually happen, and I speak *this is it people! This is not a drill!* Well, no one is going to believe me. What I have been told about timing is *when you least expect it.* Of course! Why? Patience, my dear.

There are some tasks, and lessons in those tasks. Some tests you cannot do ahead. They are, when they are. They want me to practice being the calm in the storm. It is like spirit's form of a pop quiz. "*Here are some unfortunate circumstances and we would like to see how you apply what you have learned. We will be grading you. If you pass, you get to go forward. If you do not, you get extra homework.*"

There is no doubt that I may look back and wish I were not in such a hurry to know. There is no finish line. Life is not a sprint; it is a marathon. Just stop and smell the roses. Watch the snail. Appreciate every moment as it is. Don't worry about tomorrow. Just be grateful for today, this moment, right now.

Benjamin Franklin once said, "*Time is the one currency that, once spent, you can't never earn back.*" Spend your time wisely. Patience is not just the ability to wait but to keep a good attitude while waiting. Hands down, that is my test right now. I'm not sure how good I am doing, but I am working on it and probably will be forever!

CHAPTER 40

LET'S MAKE A DEAL

Since moving, I have been getting messages from spirit that I needed to do more inner healing. I'm not going to lie; I have been avoiding it. True to form, the more I avoid something the more it pops up. The need to do shadow work was to me, like smacking me upside the head with a cast iron skillet. Not fun.

I have done *some* healing, like working on boundaries, getting my power back and letting a few things go but some of the big things needed to be addressed still. Childhood stuff. Yep, peeling it all back to the formative years. They wanted me to go deep. Bleh.

It was for the future, they said. My future. It needed to finally be done. The game I had been playing of hide-and-go-seek with my angels over this work had come to an end. They kind of laid the law of the land down for me. No more stalling for me.

I'm sure a lot of you have watched or heard of the game show *Let's Make a Deal*. Wayne Brady and other folks have hosted this long-running show for years, but the premise remained the same. You basically get a choice of three doors, each with their own prize behind them. No guarantee of what your prize is going to be, but you are going to get something. That is the only guarantee. Good? Bad? A Zonk? It is up to your choices. So, choose wisely!

They are not allowing me to bypass anything about this healing work and jump to the end. I am told repeatedly that it is not going to happen. They had a point, because when exactly is the end? Do I still look for it around every corner? Yes, I do. Easy street would be great!

Spirit is not having it. I had to do the shadow work now. Due to all my other avoidance tactics, they chose today to be the big day.

Getting back to the game show, let me paint the picture for you.

(**Announcer**) HELP ME WELCOME OUR FIRST CONTESTANT HERE ON *LET'S MAKE A DEAL* AND SAY HI TO LISA!

(**Crowd**) HI, LISA! YOU GOT THIS! WE ARE ROOTING FOR YOU!

(**Announcer**) WAYNE! TELL THE LITTLE LADY WHAT SHE COULD WIN DOING SHADOW WORK TODAY!

(The crowd waits with anticipation.)

(**WAYNE**)

"Lisa, spirit has put in front of you three doors of opportunity. Behind each door is a boat that will take you across a stretch of time. One is a cute little boat with a strong engine that will ensure your arrival to the next phase of your life unscathed. The other two boats look the same but will be Zonk-boats. They may have holes in the hull, engine issues and no paddles. They will cause you to take unfamiliar paths with more life lessons. We want you to have the best boat! Lisa, do you want the best boat?"

(*Overwhelmed, I answer yes, of course!*)

(WAYNE)

'Well, Lisa, here is your task! You have to (finally) let go of a few major things, forgive, acknowledge your lessons learned, release them, and agree to walk forward. You are never to look back. You can only go forward and embrace the future. Do so, and you are guaranteed the good boat to cross to the next phase. If you choose to not to do the work fully, you will be subjected to one of the other two boats. Now, Lisa, what do you want to do? Do the shadow work toward your healing or take a chance at getting a Zonk-boat and the unknown path?'

(*The crowd erupts with their predictions.*)

Well, I opted in to do the work. Damn, if I wanted to. Frankly the other two unknown options did not appeal to me!

What I was thinking I could get away with initially was the rush version. You know, get it over with fast! Like dropping Mentos into a two-liter bottle of pop and just spew it all and then be done right then! The work I had to do though, was going to take time. I honestly thought it would be a lot of work.

I did not think that I was holding on to it that much but obviously the signs were most definitely there that I was. Did you know that out of sight, out of mind does not equal letting it go?

Being the queen of procrastination sometimes, I realized I was still stalling about just doing it. How messed up is that? I knew I had to, but I was in a good mood and didn't want to!

So, what did I do? I tried to outrun my angels. *I'm not kidding*! Without thinking, I grabbed my purse and ran to my car. Suddenly, I found myself driving. How's that for a classic avoidance tactic? If I avoid it then it goes away, right? Oh no! Not this time!

Off in the car I went. *Have keys, will travel.* I gave myself brownie points for agreeing to *do* the long-overdue shadow work. It was a very big step for me! I just figured if I went for a drive, the timeline to do this could be pushed off to another day. Procrastination at its finest!

Ever hear the saying, "*Wherever you go, there you are*"? Well, that was me. On the other hand, my angels that watch over me had *different* ideas. It was like they all piled into the car with me and buckled their seatbelts too. They were *not* going to let this go. Talk about being a pain in the ass! I turned on the radio to drown out my thoughts they were plaguing me with and went on my merry way to anyplace else but being at home.

This next part was so wild I actually pulled over and had to write this down. You can't make this stuff up! Flipping through my radio stations to change my mental mood these songs came on in order:

Song 1: "Forgive" (didn't get the artist's name—thought it was a "coincidence")

Song 2: "Finally!" (CeCe Peniston)

Song 3: "Give It Up, Turn It Loose" (En Vogue)

Song 4: "The Best Thing That Ever Happened" (Gladys Knight)

Song 5: "Show Me Love" (Robin S)

Song 6: "I'll Wait" (Kygo)

I pictured my angels all piled in my car with crossed arms looking at me, saying, *"we can do this all day!"*

They crack me up! I so love them! Seriously, that's just funny how they do things like this! My angels were not going to let this go! They have been harping on me to do this for a *long* time. Finally saying OK wasn't enough for them. They were making sure I did the work this very day. To their credit, they must have known something I didn't to really encourage me despite my lame avoidance tactics!

I admit, the foreboding I felt about doing the work was lightened by the laughter but then came the harder part.

Doing it.

I relented and went back to my place and did what I needed to do. I felt from the heart, wrote out a gratitude letter for the lessons I learned about some very traumatic events in my life, said a few prayers through heaving sobs and released it. I burned my grief letter in my kitchen sink.

Done.

(But WAIT! There's more!)

Now, I set off the fire alarm in the apartment that is equipped with a sprinkler system! Oh my God! OK, it was four pages worth of a fire in the sink, but I didn't think it was *that* big! Simultaneously I heard some wimpy voice emanating from a small box on the wall going "fire," "fire." Seriously? That wasn't enough to wake up a hamster!

The waterworks of my tears switched off and now panic set in. Racing, I turned on the garbage disposal to dispose of the remnants of the letter. Then, I turned my attention to getting the smoke alarms to turn off before the fire department showed up or the sprinklers kicked on! Talk about the angels making me shift my energy! I did not want to have to explain all of this to a potentially hot fireman! Holy moly!

Air conditioner on full blast? Check! Ceiling fans on? Done! Doors open? Got it! Kitchen towel waving up to fan air before the sprinkler system turned on and flooded my apartment? Yes! Yes, and yes!

What-the-hell!?

When the alarm finally turned off and I heard no sound of fire trucks coming, I sat down to breathe a sigh of relief and meditate. What a day so far!

During my meditation my angels showed me the bottom of the ocean. You know, the dark part that light doesn't even penetrate where those weird-looking fish you see on nature shows live. I saw myself cutting the rope that anchored me in that dark water and, suddenly, I was shooting up toward the surface. The pretty blue water. Then, like a cork, my head was above the surface. That's how fast I shot to the top. That's also how far down I was being held by not doing the work. I couldn't even *see* the bottom anymore. Wow!

I was emotionally exhausted by this point. Holy cow. I went from intense contemplation to thigh-slapping laughter. Then heaving sobs to holy crap the fire department is going to come and I don't remember if I combed my hair! Then finally breathing a sigh of relief.

Was it enough though? I had to know! I was not going to take any chances. I wanted to make sure that I "did enough" to shift me back to the path of least resistance. I want to get in the boat that had no holes, and a strong engine to get me going forward. I did not want to have to do this again! EV-ER!

I used my phone-a-friend option and called in a favor to two of my amazing woo-woo friends. I asked them to please tap into their spirit guides. All I said to ask their guides was: *Was the release I did enough?*

Not knowing what it was even about, one of them mentioned that they saw me throwing "baggage" off a mountain cliff and it was *so far down* that all she saw was a little "dust-poof." My other friend said that she saw three doors or options for me, and the other two doors were no longer there. There was only one door for me, now.

Finally! Sheesh!

That was rough for me. *Really,* rough. I had been denying that I was holding on to a few things for a very long time. Considering that I won the boat with no holes and a sturdy engine behind door number one, I feel much better. I look forward to floating along but without any heavy stuff trying to pull me under in the future. Ties are cut. The baggage was dropped.

Briefly recalling the day's events as I crawled into bed for the night, I realized that it did not take the time I thought it would, to do the work. It was done in one day. Spirit made sure I didn't have time to wallow but put instead, a roller coaster of events in my path right after to focus on. I was not dwelling at all. I was very grateful for this.

Man, I slept like a log that night. I no longer have a rearview mirror to stare back at what was holding me down. It was gone. Shattered. Now, it is just the front windshield of my life going forward. The confusing puzzle pieces have fallen away. I still don't have a complete and clear picture of the front of the puzzle box, but I do like what I see going forward much more now. It's not a guaranteed happily ever after either, but I'm pretty sure Wayne's going to tell me there's a bonus round! Winner Winner, Chicken Dinner! WOO-HOO!

CHAPTER 41

MY SPIRIT GUIDE REVEALED

I have a stalker. Yup! This man watches my every move, oversees my daily activities and steers me on the right path unbeknownst to me. He sits in the shadows and makes sure I am safe and OK.

His name is Jean-Paul Claude.

Mind you, I don't tell him to go away. He is quiet most of the time and watches me from the wings. He only lets me know he's around when it's necessary! He is my spirit guide.

So let me back up.

At the start of my spiritual journey, I was practicing meditation. I saw pictures and words and wrote them down. I got the letter "J." No biggie. It's the tenth letter in the alphabet, and it means, what? I had no idea, but I wrote it down.

The letter came through a few times, actually. Then, I heard what sounded like "Joan," but I felt like it was a man. I then got Joen but the emphasis was on the en—like Joe-En. I had recently read a book that encouraged you to connect with your spirit guides while meditating. Was this mine? I knew no one by that name at all. So possibly? During one specific meditation, I saw piercing blue eyes that were literally inches from my face just staring at me. It actually made me jump! I truly had no clue if any of it was connected so I just continued to take notes.

I know you're saying, *"Now don't start getting all cray-cray on me."* Just hear me out! What I've learned is that our spirit guides are assigned to us at birth. We picked them out, actually! Yes, you have one of your very own, too! They are our guardians that help us out of a lot of circumstances by those nudges and gut feelings you may or may not pay attention to. They watch over you and help get the right people to reach out to you for support when you least expect it. In emergencies, they have been known to step in as well! American Indians even speak of them and are very in touch with their spirit guides.

I became aware of "Joen" coming through more often. I didn't really know he was a spirit guide at the time, so I just paid attention. Was this possibly someone I was going to meet in the future? Was this someone who had passed away and was giving me a message to give someone? I also got the word "French." Got to love pieces of the puzzle!

So, a few friends and I met up to go to the Body Mind Spirit Expo that happened to be in town. If you have never been to one, I highly suggest you go. (www.bmse.net) It is eye-opening on so many different levels being around the different metaphysical modalities all in one area! Anyway, my friends and I all opted in for different metaphysical experiences for the day. We agreed to meet up after and compare notes.

There was an intuitive artist from Virginia Beach who brings through and draws a loved one or your spirit guide. She had posted on her walls the pictures she had drawn compared to an actual photo her patrons shared with her. It was very cool! I thought, OK, I'll bite! I truly was drawn to her as were my other friends. I knew who my loved ones were in spirit and did not need that validation but my spirit guide? That stood out to me in a big way. I signed up and waited my turn.

I sat down and she introduced herself. She asked that I just chat and tell her things while she let her hand do the drawing. It puts her in the "zone." She did say that when she gets information to pass along, she would interrupt me and speak. I got my handy-dandy phone out and hit record.

She said, *tell me a story*. Without skipping a beat, I opted to tell her about this amazing book I recently had acquired from my grandfather. It's a World Almanac of sorts, but it's called *The Volume Library*.

It was first published in 1911, but my copy was from 1925. It was the Google of the early twentieth century. I told her about how I came across this book in my grandparents' attic and how it belonged to my grandfather. It was something he cherished greatly as it was purchased during the depression era at the cost of $10. Mind you, monthly wages were around $40 a month at the time, according to his memoirs.

I told her that in my channeling, I repeatedly got the message, "There is a message for you in the book." I looked and looked and had no clue. Seriously, a book from 1925 had a message for me in the 2000s? This book was already fascinating to me, but it was cool that there was some sort of a message in it for me I had yet to find.

As I rambled on about this book, the spirit-artist would interrupt me with information that my spirit guide was giving her about me. She told me I was very artistic. I assured her I liked my crayons and fingerpaints but was not nearly as talented as she was! She then drew beautiful blue eyes on this paper. *Blue eyes!*

She told me that I had a male spirit guide, and he was French. Of course, now the note from my personal channeling was front and center in my brain! I also remembered that I got the word "French." She went on to tell me that he is a musician and artist from 1857, lived in an area of France called Merce', and loved to spend time in Paris. Then she told me his name was Jean-Paul Claude.

My brain was suddenly putting pieces together from what I was told that matched what she was getting. Of course, I was also wondering if his name or information about him was in the book! With that thought, I got a major round of goose bumps! Holy cow! I was super curious but continued to listen intently as she spoke further. (I recorded this on my phone as well!)

She mentioned poetry. *"You write it as well. You are supposed to go back to it."* (I had not dabbled in poetry since high school. Interesting!) *"You like to investigate while reading—finding out stuff. You have a LOT to give people and a lot to learn but you are a fast learner. You picked him. He is the one that keeps you out of trouble, out of danger and puts you on the right path. He pulls in the other spirit guides to help you. He knows what you're up to and what you need to help you. He sometimes gets bored, so play with him. For example, ask him to coordinate all the traffic lights. He knows you sing in the car a lot. He cannot contact you, but you can contact him. He can't interfere unless you are in danger."*

Wait a cotton-pickin' minute. Did he really just tell me that I'm *boring* him? Oh, hell no! Not possible!

"Involve him a bit more. He isn't bored a lot."

(Wait, did he just read my mind?)

"Ask him to bring you the right teachers and to help you. He knows everyone in your life. He knows what you think, and he still loves you."

(GULP)

"You have to learn from your own mistakes; he can't tell you. He tells you what you need to know, not what you want to know."

As fast as it started, my portrait and reading were finished. My head was swimming with all the information I received! There he was, Jean-Paul Claude. He is my blue-eyed, French, artistic spirit guide who gets *bored* with me! In my life, it takes a lot of effort to be bored! I truly take it as a compliment! I took my picture and went to find my friends. We all shared our experiences. None of our pictures or stories were similar in any way.

I'm so glad I recorded it all! I went from being Little Miss Happy-Go-Lucky Ray of Sunshine, telling a story about my grandpa's book, to hearing about my spirit guide, what he knows about me, and that I can be *boring!* Talk about going full circle in thirty minutes or less! Jeez!

I couldn't wait to get home to the book I had of my grandfathers. I wanted to see if the information about Jean-Paul was in the history part or references of that period.

The next day, something about the name *Jean* was resonating with me. *Jean-Paul.* It popped into my head to contact my friend who speaks fluent French. I gave her the name via text and asked her to call me and pronounce it correctly, *in French.* Guess what? JEAN, when pronounced sounded just like "Joen" when spoken quickly in a French dialect. Holy cow! It's the same name! Dang! How cool was that?

Needless to say, my next project was getting out my grandfather's book. In it, I found out about a painter named Lorraine Claude, all about Merce', France, and the year 1857. Very intriguing reading for sure! Was Lorraine related to him in some way? It didn't say. Still fascinating though!

I was happy that I knew his proper name! In some of my next few meditations, I received more confirmations and very politely asked if I could call him "JP" for short. I got a yes. Woo-hoo! (Yo, Yo, Yo, JP! How you doin'?)

(Don't get your bloomers in a bunch. I joke here but I am *very* respectful!)

I gave him a certain number combination in my "signs and symbols." That way, when I get a message and that number combination shows up around it, I know it's from him!

I have the picture of JP and his beautiful blue eyes on my wall, and I say good morning to him. He doesn't make himself known all the time (no doubt because I'm *boring* at times), but he has been wonderful and sends me messages from the great beyond.

I want to point out that not all spirit guides walked the earth before. I don't know everything there is to know about JP or all angels. I have much to learn! For now, though, I'm off to see what mischief or game I can engage JP in, so he isn't *bored*!

CHAPTER 42

CHANGE OF SEASON

I t's kind of cool that you can do something repeatedly and then, one day, it's just not the same. Something different hits you. What once was shiny and new is now old and worn. Maybe it's a different smell, awareness, or mindset. Mind you, you probably did nothing different but yet, something has changed. Sometimes, it's the outside circumstances and sometimes, it's whatever is going on inside of you. It is a change of "season" and, whether we are aware of it or not, it is happening all the time.

I have been walking at my local park as I had a need to be outside for a bit. For a few miles on this particular walk, I decided to stay on the paved path instead of the dirt path. I was in la-la land walking when I noticed that there was a single leaf moving on the ground up ahead, by itself. Of course, I thought it was the wind at first. As I walked toward it, I noticed the moves were subtle, yet obvious.

Now, as you may have figured out, my mindset is that most things are heaven-sent. My angels' calling card for me is to do things that I find awe-inspiring to grab my attention. This must be one of them, right?

When I got closer, I bent down to see how this leaf was moving, only to discover that it was this little ant. One single ant was moving this big leaf all by itself. I sincerely admired its determination and willpower. It had been a long time since I had seen that in person. Why did I notice this one leaf? This one ant?

Massive trees with limbs going every which way were sprawled out in front of me. A huge number of mushrooms in all sizes and colors were all around and what I noticed was this itty-bitty ant moving a huge leaf. Was it a big sign of some sort? Not really! It was brought to my attention, though, and I looked at it in awe.

I became suddenly aware that this little ant was carrying this leaf that was 400 percent bigger than itself. One step at a time. For a moment, I felt that I wanted to pick the ant and the leaf up and put it on the other side of the road like we do with turtles sometimes. Was I putting it closer to its destination or further away from it? No clue. I opted to take a step over it and keep walking. I let the ant continue its journey.

Pondering this, I looked up and noticed a single branch of reddish-brown leaves. A single branch of them. It just stood out! It was rather pretty with its contrasting colors. I didn't think anything of it but just stared in admiration. I kept walking and then noticed random leaves fell in front of me every so often. It was then that I realized that spirit was making me aware that indeed, a change of season was coming. The signs were subtle, but the proof was all around me.

Believe it or not, I didn't have a lot of random thoughts flying through my head during this walk. I just appreciated the quiet.

(Shocking, right?) The thought lingered that things around, and in me, were indeed changing.

In a literal sense, it is getting to be *that* time of year. The fall season was starting to make an official appearance with the leaves changing colors. The kids were getting ready to start another school year. I heard the ramblings of football season starting again. Starbucks brought out their pumpkin spice latte to sell. The holidays were growing closer by the minute. Yes, it was the start of another season.

Then it hit me—*Wait, wait, wait!* Hold on a minute. Did I not just take the Christmas tree down (what seemed like) last Thursday? Is it almost time to put it up again? How fast is time flying by! I don't know about you, but normally it is not until a mass number of leaves fall that I suddenly go, *oh wow*, and pay attention to the time of year. Yet it was happening right in front of me.

I couldn't help but ponder the "seasons are changing" theme. Something about that statement had a bigger meaning to me.

Nothing stays the same. It's not like the back of a shampoo bottle where it states, *apply, lather, rinse, repeat.* (By the way, if you keep reading that, how many times should you do it?)

Things are definitely changing again. Not only for me but to and around me. The time change kicks in, and late-evening activities readjust to work with limited daylight. There are holidays and moments marked in time that we acknowledge, grieve, or celebrate. Every day, things change. Like a flag waving in front of me, another new season approaches. I think spirit was gently reminding me of this to give me a heads-up.

I know, you're saying, really? New? Yes! It is new. Are you the same person as you were last year? I think not. I know I am not. Things I thought were issues, aren't any longer. I have grown and changed and have new ways of looking at things that are different than last year. The world is different than it was last year.

Is everything going back to how it used to be? Nope! Ladies and gentlemen, we all are again, approaching uncharted territories!

So, because of this ant and leaf, this change of seasons thought has been rolling around in my head for some time.

I felt a new season of growth was approaching. The subtleness that I saw was that of a gentle reminder of things to come.

The trees do not worry when they lose their leaves. They know that shedding their old leaves, aka letting go, allows for space for new growth to happen. That tree doesn't know exactly how many new leaves will appear, just that they will (aka faith). It starts from the inside. The leaves will suddenly appear at the right time (aka divine timing).

Taking a lesson from the ant I saw on the walk, I was reminded that it found purpose for that leaf that was dropped in its path. To the ant (I assume) this was abundance, and he was ready to receive it no matter how big or small it was. The tree on the other hand was ready for new leaves, letting go of the ones from last season. It's all about perspective.

Changes are coming. Seasons are changing. No one is stuck, even if you feel like things will never change.

Just as the trees patiently await the new leaves to arrive, or the ant waits for the perfect one to fall in its path, they each are excited. Breathe.

CHAPTER 43

BACK TO SCHOOL – UNIVERSITY OF LIFE

Welcome, students, to the University of Life!

Life lessons are the course of study, and the blessings are the after-school projects.

So, what courses did you sign up for? What learning level are you in this year? Are you repeating the same class over because you didn't learn the lesson? You will recognize some familiar faces and new classmates, but the same lesson will be repeated until you are ready to move on.

The powers-that-be have explained that we all signed up for everything we are doing or getting right now *before* we came into this world. So, like it or not, *welcome back to school!*

To be honest, my report card thus far shows that I passed many courses with flying colors and got a big fat "F" on others. Those I failed, guess what? I get to do them over again!

Are we *ever* done with life-school? Nope. I think as we get older that the classroom shrinks, and the life-course-study is more of that of a "hall monitor" than a student.

Play with bad people and you get into trouble having issues and obstacles to overcome. Play with somewhat good people, learning life lessons, and you get glowing reviews because you were the star pupil. Your report card states that according to Life University guidelines, you did your course lesson right!

A lot of times, you don't even know you are in school until you look back. It's like going with the flow with the groups of people you are around. Large masses are just shuffling as one unit into another experience without notice. Then you're suddenly just in the middle of it. I think it would be like everyone trying to squeeze through the gymnasium doors for an assembly all at once. You aren't fully aware of it, but suddenly you are in the gym!

I recently came across a fourteen-page letter I wrote to my ex one week prior to filing for a divorce. Oh, I remember it like it was yesterday. I was prompted by my angelic team to write out my thoughts in a comprehensive manner in one last-ditch effort. I'm not sure if fourteen pages is rendered "comprehensive," but I had a lot to say. I was urged to write so there would be no misunderstanding about what I said or how I said it. This of course only made sense looking back. I now realize that this was my final "term paper" for this class and lessons I had to learn.

I remember going to the park with my handy-dandy notebook and pen. I figured I might as well do my homework with a view, right? I prayed for help. My great-aunt Arline came to mind. She was going to help me write what I needed to say and how to say it. My hand shot to the paper. I wrote and wrote. This was an "impromptu" writing assignment for sure. Once I turned this in, the results would let me know if I was repeating the grade or advancing.

I remember the words just flowing out of me left and right. Page after page was filled and I put them on the seat next to me in the car. What was interesting was that everything that I wrote just flowed. For an impromptu paper, I had no scratch outs and no do-overs. It was truly a one-and-done kind of paper, *in pen*. Again, there was no writing prompt. There were no notes I was reading from to guide me. Just the words in my head I heard that I put to paper.

I don't know how long it took to do but I think it was pretty fast because suddenly, I was done. I remember reading back through it. Frankly, I was disturbed how nice this letter sounded. To me it was way too polite! Just for the record, being nice was not the point I wanted to make! I thought there should be facts, figures, proof I had, and examples, to really spice it up and get my point across.

In my opinion, the point of the letter was to be up front and bold! I felt this fourteen-page letter was missing the point my heart wanted to make. What came through my pen did not convey my heart's intention as it did not pack the one-two punch impulsively, I wanted.

Who the hell wrote this? The words popped into my head, "*It's how it needs to be written to be received*" (I paraphrased it). Seriously?

I realized now that I was doing *automatic writing*. Like most things, once you look back, you see things you didn't understand while you are in the middle of it. Those are the lovely lessons of "life."

TA-DA!

My human side struggles at times with how things are to be done. My spiritual side, unfortunately, must deal with my stubborn human side *a lot*. The best way to describe my human side is like that a kindergartner who doesn't want to leave home and wants to just stay put. My spiritual side is the amazing kindergarten classroom with all sorts of friends, colored paper, scissors, and glue! Once I get there, listen and follow along, it's OK! It's just getting my stubborn ass there to get started.

Getting back to my letter, I left the park, went home, and handed it to him. Was he going to understand my viewpoint? Was he going to understand where I was coming from or read it to defend himself and his actions?

This letter was my official line in the sand. I gave him seven days to make his decision to work on our marriage and fix the issues, or we were done. His lack of a decision **was** his decision. I filed for divorce. I was done. He didn't try to stop me or give me good reason to stay.

It was interesting to come across this and read it again knowing what I know now. I now see that the letter was *amazing*. There is no question to me that I was doing automatic writing to produce this. I was in complete awe of the language used. It was well versed, written from my higher self and there was no misunderstanding about what I was trying to accomplish. It was written out of love. Taking it further with all the details, accusation and citing examples would have been lost in the translation. Funny though, I noticed I did write at the last minute one or two things at the end to make myself feel better.

I got what I needed from this class and will never go back. I passed and graduated to the next level!

Life is a classroom in and of itself. Your friends, trials, and tribulations are all part of the class you are in. Once you learn the lessons, you won't repeat them. You will simply move on.

I think the fun and happy times are like recess, winter and spring break. The buckle-down times are the classroom times. Sometimes, you just have to study, learn, and keep your nose to the grindstone so you can get the semester you are in complete and have some fun again.

We all know someone that just flat-out refuses to change, be, or do anything different than what they have repeatedly done. They are scared to change. They have this one grade or level of life figured out and they are complacent in doing it over and over again. Frankly, I understand because the unknown can be scary!

For those well-meaning people who look at you and call you nuts for trying to grow and expand, don't listen to them—listen to yourself. I look at it this way, I know I can go back and repeat a grade *if I want to*. I just relish the fact that I am not *forced* to.

Are there more classes that I need to complete? *sigh* Yes. Since life is a classroom, my angelic team wants me in a new classroom, yet again. Just like the kids are starting a new grade, a new school or university, so are we all.

There will forever be a new season, new class or if you're stuck, a repeat of something over again. Sometimes we are the teacher and sometimes the student. I think, at moments, you know which one you are. If you learn your lessons, good, bad or indifferent, you can go to the next class.

It was nice to see my old final term paper and know that I had graduated from that kind of life. It wasn't an easy lesson for me. I repeated that class, frankly, more times than I care to admit. Finally, though, I said goodbye to that teacher and fellow classmates. There was a part of me that didn't want to leave, but even my angels knew that it was going to be so much better for me to move up to the next level. I had to trust them.

Right now, I am still holding on to my hall pass. I heard the new teachers for my next level class are looking for me to get started. I wonder what I am going to learn this time. I'll meet you in the lunchroom! I heard its pizza day!

EPILOGUE

T he world was at the end of lockdown from COVID. I had run through my savings and had to make some changes fast. Reluctantly, I packed up my belongings and put them in storage leaving North Carolina with one suitcase, my spiritual gifts, and a chip on my shoulder.

Despite my pleas to spirit and absolutely *no* patience, I moved back to Florida to get on my feet again. Now, my angel wings were hiding in plain sight, and I didn't feel like I could or even wanted to fly.

Spirit handed me an empty book to pen the next part of my journey in. I had no idea what they had in mind. All they kept telling me through messages was to get comfortable being UN-comfortable and that I needed to have further experiences to learn from.

Many angels and lessons were put in my path along the way. Can I pass the pop quizzes put in front of me and walk the walk I talk?

My journey to help myself as I help others continues.

Watch for book two in the Woo-Woo series:

HIDING IN PLAIN SIGHT, Confessions of an Angel Messenger

ABOUT THE AUTHOR

LISA ANN

L isa is a prolific writer and the author of her debut book Spiritually Waking Up: You (SERIOUSLY) Can't Make This Sh*t Up! and book two in her WOO WOO Series; Hiding in Plain Sight; Confessions of an Angel Messenger.

Journaling for more than four decades, she combined her love of writing with her sense of humor and unique spin on life events. Through this palpable spark, she transformed her journey into her personal memoir to help others also going through a spiritual awakening by writing blog entries to document these hilarious events. Her relatable life and disposition shine through as she explores the importance of really getting to know yourself on a deeper level.

Through her personal unfolding she has studied with numerous mediums in the US and UK. She also attended Arthur Findlay College in England for mediumship/psychic studies. She is also a member of Rhine Research Center, at Duke University in North Carolina. Aside from her career in the real estate industry, she is also a professional psychic medium, speaker, teacher of spiritual arts, and is the former host of the podcast: MESSAGE DELIVERY! You Can't Make This Stuff Up!

Lisa spends her downtime with her family, grandchildren, and friends. She enjoys traveling, camping, scuba diving and other various adventures when she is not learning about more spiritual endeavors.

She hopes her raw and often humorous stories help you to better understand what you might also be going through so you can navigate and embrace it for your future.